Wicked
Cleveland

....

JANE ANN TURZILLO

THE
History
PRESS

Published by The History Press
Charleston, SC
www.historypress.com

All images courtesy of the Cleveland Public Library unless otherwise noted.

First published 2022

Manufactured in the United States

ISBN 9781467150248

Library of Congress Control Number: 2022933323

For John-Paul, Nicholas and Nathan, with all my love.

The fix was really in in Cleveland

—Alvin Karpis

CONTENTS

CONTENTS

ACKNOWLEDGEMENTS

This is my third book with commissioning editor John Rodrigue. It is a pleasure to work with him. His patience is appreciated, and his guidance is invaluable. Special thanks to my beta reader, Marilyn Seguin, for reading through my manuscript, making sure it all made sense and was error free. Many of the photos came from the Cleveland Public Library's Photo Collection, and I want to thank Brian Meggitt for making that process a pleasure.

Thank you to friends and fellow authors for their help: Gloria Irwin and Lisa Kaplan for advice; Casey Daniels for the "Fast Eddie" idea; Wendy Koile for tech and research help; Irv Korman for support; my brainstorming group, Julie Anne Lindsey, Cari Dubiel, Kathryn Long, Wendy Campbell and Shellie Arnold; and all my Northeast Ohio Sisters in Crime.

I also would like to thank the following people for their contributions: Chris Burton, Akron–Summit County Public Library, for help with Zoom; Judith G. Cetina, PhD, CA, Cuyahoga County Archives; Max Alan Collins and A. Brad Schwartz, authors of *Eliot Ness and the Mad Butcher*; United States marshal Peter J. Elliott, Northern District of Ohio; Natacha Faillers, archives assistant, Nevada State Library and Archives; Caryn Hilfer, *Cleveland Plain Dealer*; Rebecca McFarland, Eliot Ness expert; Russell Metcalf; and Elizabeth A. Piwkowski, Michael Schwartz Library, Cleveland State University. I hope I did not forget anyone.

This book was made possible in part by those period journalists whose bylines never appeared at the tops of their stories.

I am grateful to my son, John-Paul, my daughter-in-law, Jenn, and my grandsons, Nicholas and Nathan, for their love and support, and my sister Mary Turzillo for her confidence and encouragement.

And finally, thank you to my readers. I write these books for you.

INTRODUCTION

When I was about seven or eight, my dad worked in downtown Cleveland. My mother sometimes visited him at his office, and they would go out to lunch. Sometimes I got to go along. This was a huge treat for me.

Mother and I would usually have to wait for my dad to finish his phone calls or whatever else he was working on before we could go. This gave me the chance to visit the candy dishes on the secretaries' desks. I also liked to overhear the women's conversations. They talked about going to Short Vincent Avenue for drinks after work. They talked about meeting their boyfriends, eating at the restaurants and seeing big-name entertainers. I guess this book started way back then.

My sister, an award-winning fiction writer and poet, lived in Little Italy during the 1970s while she was getting her PhD. The Cleveland Museum of Art was close by. *The Thinker* was bombed during that time. The opening lines of her Pushcart-nominated poem about the bombing stuck in my head and are included in the chapter on that crime.

When *Ohio Heists*: *Historical Bank Holdups, Train Robberies, Jewel Stings and More* came out, one of my fellow authors, Casey Daniels, sent me an article on "Fast Eddie" Watkins. She suggested I should include him in my next book. Her dad was the head of the Cleveland police robbery division at the time Watkins held eight people hostage in a 1975 bank robbery. The case is included in this book.

One of my favorite stories from *Ohio Heists* was about Ted Conrad. He was a twenty-year-old vault teller who walked out of the bank where he worked with $215,000 in a paper sack. He disappeared until early November 2021, when a source sent me an obituary for a man named Thomas Randele. That obituary was the key to putting a fifty-two-year-old case to rest. I sent it on to U.S. marshal Peter J. Elliott at the Cleveland office, and he took care of the rest.

Cleveland is a wonderful city that sits on the southern shore of Lake Erie. It has a lot to offer its residents, surrounding suburbs and the region. It is home to world-class museums, an orchestra, a zoo, 150 parks, charming neighborhoods, ethnic villages, the second-largest theater district in the country and popular sports teams. Like every city, it also has its darker side. This book is meant to bring a few of those stories out of the shadows of history.

PART I

···

SEX, VICE AND ROCK-AND-ROLL

Chapter 1

BURLESQUE AT THE ROXY

*S*unlight shimmers on the white travertine marble of the PNC Center Bank at the northwest corner of Euclid Avenue and East 9th Street. One of Cleveland's tallest skyscrapers, the building has thirty-five stories above the ground and three below. It stands 410 feet into the city's skyline. Construction, which cost $60 million, began on the building in 1978, and it opened as the National City Bank Tower in 1980. Twenty-eight years later, PNC acquired National City.

At street level, the Center has a flower-lined pathway and a George Rickey sculpture but no evidence of the brick building that once stood on that spot or its colorful history.

In 1906, Truman M. Swetland was at the forefront of a developing industry known as moving pictures. He signed a ninety-nine-year lease with Levi E. Meacham on the property at 1882 East 9th Street in Cleveland. A year later, he opened the Family Theater and showed family films. Theaters in that day were called nickelodeons because they charged five-cent admission.

Renamed the Orpheum in 1913, it showed first-run silent films such as *Peggy* with Billie Burke and *Secret Love*, starring Helen Ware. The *Plain Dealer* wrote that the Orpheum was "one of the most comfortable downtown theaters," and it could seat six hundred viewers. A Wurlitzer provided music and sound effects that fit whatever picture was on the screen. The cost of a ticket was a quarter.

The Orpheum closed in 1929. After remodeling and redecorating, it reopened as the Roxy Theater in 1931, and by 1933, the entertainment had been transformed.

The Roxy.

Under George Young's management, the theater became a nationally known burlesque (sometimes spelled burlesk) and vaudeville house. Opening night, October 6, 1933, premiered a company of thirty entertainers, starting off with eighteen singing and dancing girls. Hal Rathbun and Benny Bernard provided laughs with their skit "Miser's Gold."

Other singers and dancers included Ruth Darling, Ann Valentine and Patricia Kelly. As an added attraction, Joanna Slade, who, according to the *Plain Dealer*, had a "Mae Westian figure and a repertory of shimmy dances," rounded out the show.

Through the years, big-name comics such as Phil Silver, Red Buttons and Bud Abbott and Lou Costello performed their routines on the Roxy stage.

During its heyday, the Roxy hosted some of the most famous burlesque queens to ever strut the stage and twirl feather boas. Red-haired Tempest Storm was a favorite of the audience, as well as a favorite date of Elvis Presley, in the '50s. Blaze Starr also performed in the '50s as Miss Spontaneous Combustion. Actress Ann Corio purportedly made $10,000 a week in the '40s, according to Alan F. Dutka, author of *Cleveland's Short*

Above, left: Tempest Storm opened at the Roxy in May 1965.

Above, right: Anna Corio performed at the Roxy.

Right: Miss Diana Midnight opened at the Roxy in April 1965.

Vincent. "The One and Only" Irma the Body peeled off almost everything with class at the Roxy. Satan's Angel performed with flaming tassels attached to the pasties on her breasts. During the '20s, Carrie Finnell held the record for the longest strip tease. She removed one item of clothing per week of her fifty-four-week run at the Roxy to reveal her ample body. She also had "educated breasts," having perfected twirling tassels attached to her pasties in different directions.

Short Vincent Avenue, which ran between East 9th and East 6th Streets, was right around the corner from the Roxy. It was a short block of bars, strip joints and restaurants. The Hollenden Hotel, a favorite for businessmen and celebrities, was at the other end of Short Vincent. This one-block-long street, the Roxy and the bar at the Hollenden made downtown Cleveland come alive with entertainment when the sun went down.

From 1968 to 1977, the Roxy's glitz and glamour began to slide, and the entertainment went from naughty to sleazy. At times, the performers and musicians outnumbered the people in the seats. The theater started showing X-rated movies and hiring strippers.

Four strippers were arrested for nudity in 1970. Cleveland vice cops claimed the girls had pulled their G-strings away during their routines. The officers waited until the end of the performance to collar the girls. Two of the women were mother and daughter. The arrest closed the show for the night.

In 1967, the court gave Kope Realty the right to take over the lease on the property for $6,000 a month. Levi Meacham, the original owner and leaseholder, died in 1920. His will stipulated that the income from the long-term lease go to Oberlin College, the Case School of Applied Science and Western Reserve. (Case and Western Reserve are now one school.) According to the will, the property was to be disposed of after the death of all Meacham's descendants, and money from the sale was to go to the colleges.

Under the new lease, Kope was supposed to tear down the old building and erect a new one by 1972 for the sum of $150,000. By 1971, construction costs had risen to the point that $150,000 would not cover a new building, so the realty company bought the property outright for $150,000.

"We're surrounded by banks and office buildings now," Jess D. Myers, manager of the Roxy at the time, told *Plain Dealer* writer William F. Miller. "This used to be an entertainment area."

Myers still wanted to keep the theater open. "This theater is our life, but it looks very, very bad." The Roxy was dealing with union problems, the sale and a declining audience.

A bomb, causing $25,000 in damages, forced the Roxy to close in September 1972. Four sticks of dynamite placed in the basement ceiling blew a four-by-five-foot hole in the lobby floor. It ripped the front door off its hinges and destroyed wiring and plumbing. Tom Flynn had become the manager only a week prior to the blast, and he had no idea who or why anyone would want to bomb the theater.

Flynn reopened the theater, but it was not the end of his problems. In 1973, the flick *Deep Throat* played at the Roxy. Flynn was arrested three times over the two days of the film's run. The city seized the three copies of the film. Later in the year, Flynn was arrested for showing *The Devil in Miss Jones*. That flick was also confiscated.

The smut detectives zeroed in on the Roxy and Flynn a few months later for showing *Behind the Green Door*, starring former Ivory Snow girl Marilyn Chambers. It was Flynn's sixth arrest. The theater's reputation was permanently tarnished.

After three years of problems with showing X-rated movies and a year of being dark, the Roxy attempted to return to live burlesque in April 1975. According to Robert Dolgan in the *Plain Dealer*, the first show featured strippers named Passion Flower, Torchy Diamond, Jayde and Gypsy Eden. They stripped down to their shoes and gloves. Barney Long was the MC. During one of his skits, he came on stage with his pants down to his knees. He tap danced, fell on his buttocks (purposely) and told corny jokes. When almost no one clapped, he said, "There will be no individual applause. Either you clap together, or you get the hell out." He said his father had appeared on the Roxy stage forty-five years before him. Presumably, his father got a better reception. There were four shows that day at a cost of six dollars each.

Things did not go smoothly for the opening. Stagehand Local 27 picketed the theater. The management said there was no need for stagehands because of the way the show was designed.

On November 6, 1977, the audience numbered just six for a showing of *Innocent Girls* and *Company Hits*. The Roxy closed its doors for good after that double feature. No more beautiful women, feathers or sequins. No more famous comics. No more bumps and grinds or shimmying. No more catcalls. No more skin flicks. No more lewd jokes. It was over. The wrecking ball was on its way to make room for a new banking center.

Chapter 2

SHORT VINCENT AVENUE

*J*ust north of where the old Roxy stood on East 9th Street is a one-block-long passageway called Short Vincent. Although it is only 485 feet long, it was once the heart of a colorful Cleveland nightlife. Tourists and celebrities mixed with bookies and mobsters for drinks, underworld gossip, a steak dinner or Coney dog and all kinds of entertainment, including "the odds on anything."

The street crossed farmland that was originally owned by a cabinetmaker and early Cleveland settler, John Vincent. As large homes were built along Euclid and Superior Avenues, the owners cut an alleyway for access to their stables and coach houses. This access alley became Vincent Avenue, Alan F. Dutka wrote in *Cleveland's Short Vincent*.

On June 7, 1885, the magnificent eight-story Hollenden Hotel opened at Superior Avenue and Bond (now East 6th Street). It was constructed of fireproof materials and had one thousand luxurious rooms, one hundred private baths and electric lights. Rooms were available for travelers and permanent residents. Lavish decorations included crystal chandeliers and wood paneling. The hotel's swanky Crystal Restaurant was a favorite gathering place for politicians, bankers and industry giants. Five presidents dined there. It had a barbershop with a phone at each chair. During the '40s, the elegant Vogue Room featured well-known entertainers, as well as upstart Dean Martin.

The hotel's back door opened onto Vincent Avenue, setting the stage for commercial development. Soon the short block was alive with restaurants,

Short Vincent Avenue.

Street view of Short Vincent Avenue.

Hotel Hollenden.

bars and a host of entertainment and businesses that served the guests of the hotel and Cleveland at large.

As Vincent Avenue became more developed, gambling, prostitution and even murder followed. The *Plain Dealer* reported the murder of "Roughhouse" John Murphy at the Oak Café. Murphy and Leonard A. "Lenny" Lyons had a long-standing feud. The men were "cappers" (go-

Safety director Edwin D. Barry with policeman Louis Mlakar, circa 1928.

betweens for gamblers) for competing gambling houses. Their rivalry finally got into a deadly altercation on August 20, 1917. Lyons shot Murphy three times in the abdomen. (As Murphy lay dying on the floor, someone stepped up to steal his cufflinks and then vanished out the door.) Lyons escaped before police got to the scene but later turned himself in with his brother's assistance.

"It was Murphy's life or mine," Lyons said at his arrest. Lyons was convicted of manslaughter and sentenced to prison for one to twenty years.

When it came to gambling, the city's safety director, Edwin D. Barry, ordered a sweep of businesses, concentrating on poolrooms, cigar stores, laundries and men's clothing stores. Undercover detectives visited suspicious shops and businesses and placed bets with marked or previously recorded bills. Later, during raids, they found and were able to identify the bills in cash registers, proving gambling and business monies were mixed. Police confiscated racing forms and betting tickets marked with initials, odds and horses' names.

Captain Martin J. Gaul and his "roving gambling squad" closed 129 houses in Greater Cleveland and made 3,300 arrests in 1924 alone. Suspects were fingerprinted, photographed and measured with the Bertillon system.

A cigar store at 814 Vincent Avenue was the target of one of these raids in August 1925. Police were determined to put the owner, Dan Sanders, out of business because he had managed to dodge accountability. One of the eight officers in on the raid ran afoul of Ohio Court of Appeals chief justice Manuel Levine, who was at the store to buy some smokes. None of the officers recognized Levine. As the judge paid for his cigars and turned to leave, one of the eight demanded his name. He refused to give it. The officers threatened to arrest him and call the wagon. Levine told the policeman and his superior if they laid a hand on him, he would have them arrested. Bystanders knew who he was and called police headquarters. Police brass quickly cleared it up.

Gambling continued in one form or another into the 1990s. Scalping Browns' and Indians' tickets became a business, and Short Vincent (as it became known in the early '30s due to creative press agent Mitchell Dexter Plotkin) was the place to find a ticket. All one needed to do was leave a name at enough places up and down the street, and a ticket would show up. If an event was sold out, someone along the street could produce tickets, often at a much higher price. The *Plain Dealer* wrote that some hotel employees even handled tickets. One visitor to the area paid fifty dollars for two five-dollar tickets. Even when the Indians limited two tickets to a person, bars along Short Vincent Street were selling sheets of tickets.

Strip joints, clip joints, restaurants and other businesses moved in and out of the neighborhood like a revolving door. By 1944, there were no fewer than fifteen bars on the one-block street. The more respectable establishments moved to the north side of the street. The seedier bars and entertainment kept to the south side. The roadbed that divided the two sides was called the Gaza.

CLUB CARNIVAL, CLUB CAROUSEL AND GEORGE'S BAR

Norman Khoury worked his way up from a bartender during the Depression to owning multiple bars in the '40s and '50s—three of them in the Great Lakes Brewery building on the southwest corner of East 9th Street and Short Vincent. Club Carousel faced East 9th, and Club Carnival and George's Bar faced Short Vincent. The three bars worked under the same liquor permit and shared a kitchen.

Both Club Carousel and Club Carnival attracted police and state liquor agents' attention throughout their existence. Club Carousel offered a "Non-Stop Marathon of Beauties on Parade" and lost its liquor license for a short time after a Cleveland detective claimed one of the striptease acts was vulgar. It regained the right to pour booze after eight police, including a policewoman, saw nothing corrupt. Even Floyd Gable, the district liquor enforcement officer, saw no harm.

Years later, Gable switched careers and became the manager of the Club Carnival. He replaced the mob-connected manager Salvatore "Sam" Poliafico, who went to prison for selling two ounces of heroin to a gambler, James J. Mandanici.

Above: Club Carousel and George's, owned by Norman Khoury at the corner of East 9th Street and Short Vincent Avenue, 1950s.

Left: Club Carousel on East 9th Street.

Norman Khoury, owner of Clubs Carousel and Carnival and George's.

During the '40s and '50s, joints on the south side of the street employed B-girls (bar-girls) who encouraged men to buy them expensive cocktails. B-girls often posed as secretaries who stopped by the bar for a drink after work. Bartenders served the girls heavily watered-down drinks (usually vodka) and kept tabs on their commission. The more experienced girls could down several drinks in an evening and make a tidy sum. Of course, this was in violation of the liquor laws, so bartenders kept a sharp eye out for liquor agents.

In 1955, Club Carnival, Club Carousel and George's Bar were put under suspension for B-girls' activities, and Khoury's appeals went nowhere. More trouble followed at Khoury's Circus Club on East 12th Street, where a seventeen-year-old girl, calling herself "Boots King," unknowingly solicited a liquor control agent. "Boots" was sent to the detention home. At the end of that year, Khoury closed all three of his Short Vincent bars.

FROLICS CAFÉ

After Club Carnival vacated 814 Vincent Avenue, Frolics Café moved in. One of Frolics' owners was Charles J. Pollizzi, son of numbers racketeer and tax evader Charles A. "Chuck" Pollizzi. The younger Pollizzi left Frolics in 1959. A few years later, he tried his hand at bank burglary. He and two others tried to relieve the Cleveland Trust Company on Broadway, SE, of its assets. Things did not go as planned, and Pollizzi, who was the lookout for the job, and his two pals were arrested.

Former racketeer Angelo "Big Ang" Lonardo had a hand in ownership of Frolics after Pollizzi left, but Max Brook was the principal stockholder.

The clientele did not improve under the new management. B-girls grew more aggressive and careless with whom they approached. Prostitutes were also a problem, as they knew Frolics was a good place to pick up johns. Sometimes prostitutes and B-girls were one and the same. On

Left: Charles J. Pollizzi, owner of Frolics Café at 814 Vincent Avenue.

Right: "Big Angelo" Lonardo had a hand in the ownership of Frolics.

separate occasions in 1963, barflies Toni Venice, Taffy Twist and Flavora unknowingly approached liquor control agents. The girls all had the same come-on: a twenty-five-dollar bottle of champagne and "I'm yours for the rest of the night."

The management claimed the hookers did not work for the bar; instead, they were independent contractors provided by an agency. Liquor control did not buy that excuse. It revoked Frolics' license, but the bar stayed open anyway.

In 1964, bartender Leo Trankito beat a customer to death. According to the *Plain Dealer*, Al Furman, an Akron man, was a regular. On March 7, Furman started drinking around 11:00 p.m. At 1:00 p.m., he became so belligerent that Trankito showed him the door. Furman returned a bit later with a loaded gun and pointed it at Trankito. Another bartender, Norman Haddad, stepped in and talked Furman into putting the weapon away and going to the Town Pump bar around the corner. Haddad went with him. When Haddad did not return, Trankito went to look for him. At Town Pump, Furman pulled his gun again and aimed it at Trankito. Trankito punched Furman and knocked him against the bar. Haddad grabbed the gun and took it back to Frolics. But that was not the end of the fight. Trankito and Furman exchanged more blows, and Furman was

Prostitutes and B-girls operated freely at Frolics Bar.

knocked unconscious. Trankito carried him out to the sidewalk and left him. Furman died of head injuries later. Both bartenders were charged in the death, but it was ruled a justified homicide.

By 1964, Frolics had racked up so many offenses that it closed.

MICKEY'S LOUNGE

Mickey's Lounge at 732 Short Vincent was owned by Charles "Fuzzy" Lakis and Mickey Miller, a couple of guys with less than stellar reputations. Lakis was the worse of the two, with convictions for gambling and bookmaking. Miller had his own problems with operating a couple of gambling establishments. Although he was a co-owner of the Theatrical Grill, he also operated several dodgy bars downtown.

With Lakis's and Miller's reputations, it was no wonder Mickey's Lounge was under constant surveillance and in hot water with the Ohio State Board of Liquor Control. Early on, Mickey's and other neighborhood

Mickey's, owned by Charles "Fuzzy" Lakis and Mickey Miller, was always in hot water with liquor control.

joints drew license suspensions from the liquor board for not serving food, a provision in state liquor licenses. Mickey's kitchen fared a bit better than some of the others with a can of spaghetti soup and some crackers in the larder. "We go to Kornman's," a barmaid explained, referring to a white-tablecloth steak and chop restaurant with good food down the street. The bar stayed open while Lakis fought the fifteen-day suspension for two years. He eventually lost the battle.

In 1955, the Board of Liquor Control charged the bar with serving an already inebriated patron two shots of whiskey. A test tube containing a sample of the booze went missing before the hearing. It might have been an embarrassment to the authorities, but the chief chemist had already analyzed it, and the barmaid admitted selling the drinks.

Management ignored warnings to post drink prices, and citations for allowing B-girls to solicit alcohol piled up at Mickey's.

The state liquor chief, an agent and a *Plain Dealer* reporter visited Mickey's one evening and were immediately approached by a woman asking to join them. When they turned her down, she became verbally abusive. A bit later, another woman with a story of being from "the old country" approached them. The men denied her request also. A third woman calling herself Nadine became physically abusive when the men showed no interest. At that, the barmaid called out to them, "Why don't you buy Nadine a drink?" That was solicitation, and the agents wrote a citation.

In the fall of 1961, Lakis's liquor license expired. A few months later, he was found guilty of using B-girls to solicit drinks from patrons. The state liquor board refused to renew Mickey's license on the grounds of the B-girls' conduct and solicitations.

Lakis later drew fines and contempt of court charges. Finally, after four years of legal battles, Mickey's closed for good.

PONY'S AND 730 LOUNGE

Harry Weinzimmer earned the nickname "Pony Boy" because he had a fondness for gambling on horse races. In 1924, he had a run-in with the "roving gambling squad" headed by Cleveland police captain Frank O. Smith. Weinzimmer owned a cigar store with some questionable back-room dealings with bookies and other lowlifes. When Smith and two patrolmen raided the cigar store, Weinzimmer tried to swallow a betting slip. One of the cops grabbed him by the neck and forced him to cough it up.

Pony Boy had a nasty temper, as evidenced by his use of a blackjack on a customer at the Palais D'Or on Woodland Avenue, where he worked for a time. He then threatened to kick the teeth out of the victim's wife. After that, Cleveland's public safety director, Edwin D. Barry, told Weinzimmer to leave town and never come back, but Weinzimmer did not follow that advice.

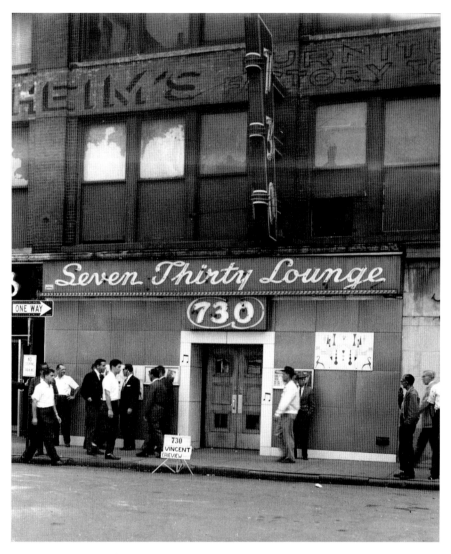

The 730 Lounge on Vincent Avenue next to Pony's collected several liquor violations.

Weinzimmer opened a bar at 732 Short Vincent and named it Pony's. He died two years after opening the bar, and his half brother, Leonard Cohen, took it over. Cohen also ran the 730 Lounge, named for the address. Both Pony's and the 730 Lounge collected an array of violations for soliciting, furnishing liquor to minors and Sunday sales. In one two-year period, the two bars collected twenty-seven citations and were in and out of court almost constantly. They were also cited for failure to serve hot meals. When

Harry "Pony Boy" Weinzimmer owned Pony's at 732 Vincent Avenue.

agents paid a visit to the kitchen at the 730 Lounge, all they found was a jar of cherries in the refrigerator and a box of potato sticks.

The 730 Lounge was sold in 1971 to Walter Abraham, the retired UAW Local 1050 president. Three years later, his brother, Charles, was indicted for attempting to bribe Cleveland patrolman Scott Manley with $50 to not arrest a woman who had peeled off her blouse and began dancing suggestively in the lounge. She was arrested for nudity. Charles was fined $250 and put on probation for two years.

After that, National City Bank bought the building and went to court to evict the bar. The bank claimed the lounge permitted lewd activity and illegal sales of alcohol. In its suit, the bank said it had asked the bar to vacate the premises, but the lounge owners refused. National City won.

THEATRICAL GRILL

The Theatrical Grill was a mainstay and probably the most infamous stop on Short Vincent. Morris "Mushy" Wexler and his brother-in-law Micky Miller opened the "jazz joint"/restaurant as Micky's Theatrical Grill in a ninety-year-old former brewery in 1937. In no time, it became the place to be—the place where entertainers ate and drank alongside gangsters, newspapermen and sports figures. Marilyn Monroe, Lauren Bacall,

Edward G. Robinson and Judy Garland spent time there. Frank Sinatra, Tony Bennett, Andy Williams and Perry Como sang there. Jimmy Durante and Milton Berle told jokes there. It was a favorite of sports figures such as Joe DiMaggio, Joe Louis and Rocky Colavito, as well as Art Modell, Nick Mileti and Don King. Modell closed the $4 million deal to buy the Browns at the Theatrical in 1961.

Any night of the week, mob bosses, underworld figures and bookies were eating dinner and conducting business at the Theatrical. Mobster Alex "Shondor" Birns "swaggered about Short Vincent Street with a big cigar in his mouth," said Democratic prosecutor hopeful Richard H. Miller, Esq., to the *Plain Dealer* in 1964. The Theatrical was Birns's "headquarters," where he had his own table. Birns's arch enemy, Danny Greene, also socialized at the restaurant, but the two knew the Theatrical was "strictly neutral territory." Notorious Cleveland mob boss Jack Licavoli never drank, but he hung out at the Theatrical.

Wexler ran the Empire Wire Service that kept bookies apprised of horse lineups and sports. Not only did a Senate committee accuse him of being a member of the Cleveland mob, but the IRS was constantly looking at him, as was the Liquor Control Board. The IRS handed him a $59,806 bill for his share of 1949 winnings of $708,000 he mixed with his bookie. At one point, Wexler owned one of the largest horse stables in the country but was banned from horse races for drugging one of his entries.

The Theatrical was destroyed by a grease fire on September 13, 1960.

Determined to hang on to his customers while his restaurant was being rebuilt, Wexler rented a corner bar in the Hollenden Hotel. The new, bigger and more opulent restaurant included meeting rooms, a kidney-shaped bar and a second floor. During the reconstruction, Short Vincent bookies took odds on whether the Theatrical would meet the opening deadline. It opened in October 1961.

In 1965, Wexler stepped away from the day-to-day business, leaving it in the hands of his son-in-law, Irving "Buddy" Spitz. Birns was not happy with the changes and dissolved his "silent" partnership. Wexler finally retired to his farm in Solon, which grew and supplied vegetables to the Theatrical Grill.

Art Modell closed the deal to buy the Browns at the Theatrical Grill.

Above: The Theatrical Grill on Vincent Avenue burned down in 1960 but was rebuilt by Morris "Mushy" Wexler.

Opposite, top: James Licavoli (*right*) with his attorney, Dominick J. "D.J." Lapolla (*left*).

Opposite, bottom: Morris "Mushy" Wexler rebuilt the Theatrical Grill after the 1960 fire.

Wexler died in 1979. In 1987, fire closed the restaurant for a second time, but it reopened within a few weeks. Management tried to keep its old customers while attempting to attract a newer, younger crowd. In 1992, Jim Swingos rented the Theatrical but did not draw enough business to pay the bills. By then, Cleveland's nightlife had moved to the flats, and the Theatrical was the only building that was not a parking lot left on Short Vincent.

The Theatrical was sold again and became a comedy club, then a sports bar and finally a gentlemen's club with pole dancers as entertainment.

It closed for good in 1999 and was demolished to make way for a parking lot. It was the longest-running jazz club in the city.

Chapter 3

JEAN'S FUNNY HOUSE
PEEP SHOWS

*J*ean's Funny House was in a former blacksmith shop on the corner of 1773 East 9th Street and Walnut Avenue. Although it was not on Vincent Avenue, it was down the street from the Roxy and fit right in with the neighborhood. At its most popular, it was a magnet to kids who loved to buy novelties like whoopie cushions, rubber vomits, magic tricks, joy buzzers and a host of other things. Party favors like party poppers, hats, masks and blowout noisemakers were popular with both kids and adults. A live monkey charmed the clientele.

The first owner of the shop was seventeen-year-old Claude Hale, who opened his business in 1914, according to author Alan F. Dutka. At first, Hale sold confectionaries, but after a while, he started displaying his collections of weaponry. He also found an audience for gruesome pictures of auto accidents. Gradually, he added novelties.

Angelo and Gertrude Gervaras purchased Hale's store in 1932 and continued to build the business—not always for the better. At one time, the store had 350 arcade games. Youngsters hung out to play the games. They slid their nickels and dimes into pinball machines and pistol games. When they thought no one was looking, they spent their quarters on two-minute peep shows that featured lingerie-clad women.

From 1937, Jean's Funny House was on the police radar. Eliot Ness was one of the first safety directors to obtain a conviction because of a horse-race slot machine at the store. That crime drew a fifty-dollar fine and a ten-day suspended sentence.

Jean's Funny House at 1773 East 9th Street.

Sometime later, Angelo Gervaras found himself in hot water with police for having $5,000 worth of obscene literature on the shelves. Gervaras insisted that he was a good man who gave $500 to the Red Cross and always bought tickets for police and fire department dances. He claimed he did not read half the literature that came into the store. He assured authorities he would have taken the material down if police requested him to. The charge was a felony and carried a $2,000 fine and five-year prison sentence.

During a 1943 police raid on the funhouse, detective Edward J. Flanagan viewed fifty-two peep shows and seized eight pinball machines. Gervaras was let off the hook when he agreed to replace the shows with police-approved entertainment.

He was not so lucky in 1954, when he was indicted for income tax evasion. According to the *Plain Dealer*, he dodged more than $120,000 in taxes during a three-year period. He served three years in a federal penitentiary.

While Gervaras was in prison, his wife, Gertrude, faced her own legal problems. In *Cleveland's Short Vincent*, author Dutka wrote that she was arrested in 1958 for hosting obscene peep shows in the store. She appealed her conviction several times but lost. She served a year in the women's reformatory.

By 1963, Jean's Funny House had a back room with a sign over the door that read, "No Minors Allowed." Twenty-five-cent, two-minute flicks with

Police raided Jean's Funny House and removed objectionable slot machines.

such titles as *Tiger Girl*, *Horsing Around* and *Girly Show* were featured in that back room. Front-room peep shows starring lingerie-clad women cost a nickel or a dime. One of the opinion pieces on the May 3, 1963 editorial page of the *Plain Dealer* described the movies as sordid, tawdry and a public nuisance. It concluded by saying, "It's time to close it up for good!"

Once again, the police viewed the movies but found that they were no worse than what was being shown at the Roxy. Detectives said the flicks did not violate Ohio's obscenity laws.

Angelo Gervaras retired in 1966 and died in January 1968. The one-hundred-year-old building along with the Gilsey Hotel next door met the wrecking ball to make room for the Ohio Savings Plaza.

The Gervarases' son, Gregory, reopened Jean's Funny House across the street. It survived for a decade before being torn down for another bank building.

Chapter 4

CLOSING DOWN
THE HARVARD CLUB

By the 1930s, gambling had a strong hold on Cuyahoga County and the city of Cleveland. The Harvard Club in Newburgh Heights—the largest gambling club between New York City and Chicago—and the Thomas Club in Mayfield Heights were known to be mob-owned and dependent on police protection.

The clubs operated with rigged equipment, marked cards and loaded dice, cheating players out of thousands of dollars. Complaints piled up from wives whose husbands gambled away the rent, the grocery money or the money for babies' shoes. Even more tragic, men committed suicide after losing everything to fixed poker games.

In January 1936, Cuyahoga County prosecutor Frank T. Cullitan, fifty-six, had a plan to shut down both clubs and arrest the owners all in one night, but he had to act discreetly. As long as "Honest John" Sulzmann, a proponent of "home rule," was Cuyahoga County sheriff, both clubs could operate with open disregard for the law.

At 3:00 p.m. on January 10, Cullitan hired twenty men from the McGrath Detective Agency and arranged to have them sworn in as special constables at the Cleveland Heights Justice Center by Justice of the Peace Joseph C. Calhoun. Calhoun handed Cullitan two sets of warrants to search the two clubs and seize all gambling equipment. Cullitan requested and received warrants for Harvard Club owners James "Shimmy" Patton, Dan Gallagher and Arthur Hebebrand and Thomas Club owners Davie Miller, Sam "Gameboy" Miller and Alex "Alky" Miller, three brothers. Cullitan also had

Prosecutor Frank T. Cullitan with guns used to commit crimes.

in hand John Doe warrants for any operators. Lastly, he hired two vans to haul away the gambling equipment.

Once Cullitan had his team assembled, he split them into two raiding parties. He and his assistant prosecutor Thomas A. Burke Jr. would take half of the newly sworn-in constables and a set of warrants to the Thomas Club on the corner of Thomas and McCracken Roads in Maple Heights. Cullitan directed his chief assistant prosecutor Charles J. McNamee, John J. Mahon, Frank D. Celebreeze and detective sergeant Patrick J. Ryan to raid the Harvard Club at 3111 Harvard Avenue in Newburgh Heights.

The two squads left the Cleveland Heights Justice Center at 4:00 p.m. McNamee arrived at the Harvard Club by 5:00 p.m. and pounded on the door. He recognized "Shimmy" Patton, who answered the door and allowed just McNamee to step inside. "I have warrants to search this place and arrest you and the other operators," McNamee said.

Patton was a pugnacious, fat little man who glued his black hair back with pomade. He told McNamee to "get out" or he would "get hurt," then pointed to a balcony that circled the edge of the building, where heavily armed lookouts stood ready. "If any of those guys you have with you try to get in here, we'll mow 'em down."

The club was humming with at least one thousand men and women at the gaming tables, so McNamee knew there would be bloodshed if he ordered his men to storm the club. He backed off to wait for Cullitan.

In the meantime, Cullitan and Burke were more successful at the Thomas Club. A lookout met them at the door. Cullitan showed him the warrant. The lookout told them to wait while he went to speak to someone inside before he could open the door. After ten minutes or so, Cullitan and his men grew impatient. They picked up a nearby bench and used it as a battering ram to break down the door. Someone suddenly pulled it open before it was completely knocked in.

Charles J. McNamee.

The room was full of people; curiously enough, many were older women. The gaming operators had left their tables to mingle with the patrons so they could not be identified and arrested. Cullitan allowed the patrons to cash in their chips before his men forced all of them to leave the building.

According to the *Plain Dealer*, the raiders confiscated three roulette wheels, thirteen slot machines, seven craps tables and four chuck-a-luck cages (a game of chance played with three dice inside a spinning cage) and loaded them into a van.

The constables busted the lock on the office door and entered. They seized $1,000 in silver change and confiscated a .22-caliber revolver, a sawed-off shotgun, a tear gas pistol, a blackjack and a large knife. They moved the desk along with two safes, a telegraph switch panel and key and a loudspeaker system used to announce race results to the van. There was so much gambling equipment and paraphernalia that the van needed to make two trips.

After closing down the Thomas Club, Cullitan and his team sped over to the Harvard Club, arriving shortly after 7:00 p.m. Cullitan encountered Patton outside the building, pacing up and down, spewing curse words. The squat little man was wearing a green hat, black overcoat and white scarf around his neck that floated in the cold wind.

Above: Frank T. Cullitan (*left*) and Thomas A. Burke Jr. (*right*) with confiscated gambling devices.

Opposite: Harvard Club owner James "Shimmy" Patton.

The two men had a sharp exchange in which Cullitan tried to be diplomatic and Patton continued to curse and threaten. The *Plain Dealer* provided some of the conversation (expletives deleted).

"Anyone that goes in there gets their ---- --- head knocked off. You've got your ------- home at stake and we got our ------- property at stake," Patton yelled.

Cullitan answered, "I've tried every decent way I could…"

"No, you haven't," Patton cut him off.

"This is my job to close this place."

"Why don't you quit your job?" Patton shot back.

"I've tried to go about this as decently as I could and we're going to see it through."

Cullitan retreated to the gas station across the street, where the men huddled against the cutting Lake Erie winds. He used the station's phone to call Cleveland police and ask for two squads of men to back him up. Acting detective inspector Joseph Sweeney said he would have to think it over, citing jurisdictional issues.

As Cullitan slammed down the phone, a man who called himself Joe approached. "We'll let you in as soon as we get our money counted. We ain't going to 'double' you."

Just then, the lights in the parking lot went out. It got very dark, but the raiders could make out cars being loaded up with gambling equipment and driving away. Cullitan could not confiscate any of that equipment, as his warrant was for evidence inside the building, not on the outside. Cullitan consoled himself with thinking they had at least shut the place down.

As the cars pulled out of the lot, the thirty-nine-year-old, ruddy-complected Art Hebebrand appeared with Patton. The two began to talk with McNamee, Celebreeze, Mahon and Ryan. A newsman tried to eavesdrop on the conversation, but Patton hollered at him to "get out of here." The reporter was able to hear Patton shout at McNamee, "You ain't going to make a pinch here. No pinches! Understand!"

Newsmen and curiosity seekers braved the cold to witness what was going on. Cullitan was becoming desperate. He called the county jail and asked for deputies to be sent. Chief jailer William J. Murphy said he would have to check with Sheriff Sulzmann, who was home sick.

Harvard Club owner
Arthur Hebebrand
(*right*).

Sulzmann said Cullitan should call Newburgh Heights mayor Jerry Sticha in order to have deputies ordered out for assistance, "in accordance with my home rule policy," the sheriff said. The mayor was unavailable when Cullitan tried to reach him.

Cullitan then called the central police station and asked to speak to Chief George J. Matowitz but failed to reach him. He left messages for the chief at the station and his home.

"This is the most brazen defiance of law and order I have ever heard of anywhere. This is going to be a showdown," Cullitan said. He had one last recourse: Cleveland's safety director, Eliot Ness.

Called out of a meeting, Ness listened to Cullitan's predicament. He committed to helping, but there was a problem. Once he stepped out of the city limits, he knew he had no authority. He tried calling Sulzmann and got the same runaround as Cullitan.

Next, he went to talk to Cleveland's mayor, Harold H. Burton, and the law director. After that conversation, he determined that although he could not

Eliot Ness (*left*) with Frank T. Cullitan (*right*).

act in his official capacity, he could act as a private citizen in order to provide security to Cullitan. He took police officers with him but first made sure they understood they were to act as private citizens guarding the prosecutors. He went to central station at shift change, where, according to the *Plain Dealer*, four plainclothes men, ten motorcycle officers and twenty-nine uniformed patrolmen were happy to join him.

Armed with shotguns, revolvers and teargas pistols, they arrived at the Harvard Club just after 10:00 p.m. Their path was blocked at first by what Ness called "tough-looking birds." He ordered the driver to hit the sirens and move through the crowd.

After Ness let Cullitan know he was there to act as protection, he made himself known to the press. Unarmed, Ness, bundled in a camel-colored coat with a black fedora on his head, led the heavily armed troops right up to the front door and met no resistance. Ness shoved the door open.

After almost six hours, Cullitan, McNamee and the constable could serve their warrants. They were faced with a huge, empty gambling hall.

Police at the door of the Harvard Club.

Everything had been stripped, except for a few betting slips on the floor, some dice tables and a race chart. They found ledger sheets and betting forms in the storeroom and some personal effects. They confiscated what was left and arrested twenty gangsters. One gangster they hoped might be there was Public Enemy No. 1, Alvin Karpis. Karpis was known to frequent the Harvard Club and even work as an enforcer for the owners from time to time. But if he had been there that day, he was long gone.

Ness noticed a hole in the ceiling that was covered with a square piece of bulletproof glass. He pulled down a ladder from the ceiling and climbed up for a look. He found a strong room with holes for machine guns in case of a robbery or raid.

"Shimmy" Patton was nowhere to be seen. One of the cops found Arthur Hebebrand and was about to arrest him. When Hebebrand was presented with a warrant, he made some threats to the arresting officer but said he would get his coat from the office. Once in the office, he closed and locked the door and then dragged a chair to the window and climbed out.

Right before leaving the scene, Cullitan and Ness noticed a sign on the wall notifying patrons of a limousine service to and from locations around the city—one of them was Cleveland Heights City Hall.

A month later, the Harvard Club reopened at 4209 Harvard Avenue and continued to operate amid police raids, grand jury investigations and even changes in ownership. Finally, in 1941, Judge Frank J. Lausche ordered it to close. When the club continued to operate in defiance of the order, Detective Captain Michael Blackwell and Cleveland police moved in and shut it down for good.

Chapter 5

W.O.W.

Wendy Orlean Williams (W.O.W.) earned the nickname "queen of shock rock" as the lead singer of the punk rock band the Plasmatics. She had a voice like a rusty power tool grinding on a single note and a love of pyrotechnics and chainsaws.

"Ever since I was little, I liked to smash things," she said in an interview in New York. "I hate conforming. I hate people telling me what to do. It makes me want to smash things."

One of her best-known stunts was punctuating a Plasmatics concert by crashing and burning a Cadillac before an audience of six thousand. In another concert, she spray-painted a four-letter word on a car, beat it with a sledgehammer and then blew it up—all on stage. Expensive guitars were sliced in two with chainsaws, and televisions were pulverized with sledgehammers.

The band formed in 1976 with Rod Swenson as its manager and began recording on the StiffAmerica record label. As the band grew in popularity, Williams and the guitarists wore more and more outlandish garb. Lead guitarist Richie Stotts, who was a towering six feet, seven inches, wore a blue mohawk and either a nurse's uniform or maid's uniform with a crinoline sticking out from under a short skirt and fishnet hose. Rhythm guitarist Wes Beech painted black designs on his sneering face and opted for either a black leather vest or a black cut-away jacket with tails. Bassist Jean Beauvoir chose a formal pure white tux and thin white sunglasses to match his white mohawk. Williams changed her blond hair to a black mohawk with blond

Wendy O. Williams of the Plasmatics with bassist Chris Romanelli. *Author's collection*.

The Agora on East 24th Street.

shaved sides. Her onstage costumes—if you could call them that—became more and more revealing until they got down to a few inches of bikini bottoms and strips of shiny black tape over her nipples. She added either shaving or whipped cream to her ensemble.

This outfit did not go over too well with Cleveland vice detectives when the band played at the Agora at 1730 East 22nd Street and East 24th Street on January 21, 1981.

The guitars blasted on one ear-splitting chord as Williams screamed the word "squirm" from a tune (if you could call it that) of the same name and some indistinguishable lyrics from "Test Tube Babies," two songs from the band's latest album. As she sang, she bounced up and down. In between her vocals, she strutted around the stage and took a chainsaw to a guitar and television set and a sledgehammer to an amplifier. Apparently, she did something with a sledgehammer that eight vice cops who viewed the concert thought was obscene. She had been arrested at a prior concert in Milwaukee for similar choreography.

After the performance in Cleveland, Williams collapsed and got a ride to the hospital, where doctors said she was exhausted and needed rest, so she and the band laid over at the Holiday Inn at East 22nd Street and Euclid Avenue. The next day, police arrested her and charged her with pandering obscenity, a first-degree misdemeanor with a maximum penalty of six months jail time and $1,000 fine. The courtroom was packed when Williams appeared before the judge wearing a black leather jacket and red skintight pants.

Police said when she first came on stage, she was wearing a white top and shorts but later stripped down to the bikini, tape and whipped cream. "She did a sado-masochistic dance using the microphone," the complaint read.

Williams was released on $200 bond. "Women should have the same rights as men. If a man took off his shirt, no one would arrest him," she said. After calling the charges "a colossal waste of tax payers' money," she flew to New York with her bandmates.

She returned to Cleveland in April 1981 for the trial. The jury of middle-aged men and women viewed a tape of her performance and heard testimony of the vice detectives.

After two hours of deliberation, the jury found her not guilty. The jury forewoman, Helen Bartnicki, said there was no question that she did the acts. "But it was a matter of deciding whether the community in this day and age had changed enough to accept it. As long as there was a shadow of a doubt, we couldn't convict her." She said they all agreed they would not want to see the show.

Williams leapt to her feet and blew a kiss to the jury. "Thank you so much," she said. "There is still a matter of choice in this country, and why should Cleveland be any different?" She went on to call prosecutors "the real whores in this. It's an obscene waste of money."

In 1985, she mounted a solo career and went on to be nominated for a Grammy. Two years later, she rejoined the Plasmatics. In 1991, she and her manager/companion Rod Swenson retired to Storrs, Connecticut, where she worked in animal rehabilitation.

After battling depression for several years, Wendy O. Williams died by a self-inflicted gunshot wound in April 1998. She was forty-eight.

PART II

COPS, CORPSES AND CROOKS

Chapter 6

THE ASSASSIN

On September 5, 1901, William McKinley, the twenty-fifth president of the United States, visited the Pan American Exposition in Buffalo, New York. Just a few months into his second term, he was there to speak to a record crowd of 116,000 on "America's role in the world." The public was invited to meet-and-greet the president at the Temple of Music theater at 4:00 p.m. the next day.

McKinley's staff and his personal secretary, George B. Cortelyou, worried about the president's safety during the function. Cortelyou had tried to cancel the event twice, but the president enjoyed meeting his constituents and would not hear of canceling. Apprehensive, Cortelyou requested to have more police and soldiers added to the usual Secret Service detail.

On that sweltering afternoon of September 6, an organist played a Bach sonata in the background as men and women patiently waited in a long line for a chance to shake the president's hand. Guards became concerned when one man shook the president's hand and lingered longer than normal. His actions distracted their attention from the next person in line, a twenty-eight-year-old man from Cleveland named Leon Frank Czolgosz (pronounced *Chol-gosh*). His intent was far different than the other people waiting to greet the president. Czolgosz had a .32-caliber gun hidden by a handkerchief wrapped around his right hand and concealed in his pocket.

When it was Czolgosz's turn, he stepped up to the president, who smiled at him, bowed slightly and offered his hand. At 4:07 p.m., Czolgosz yanked his right hand with the gun from his pocket, thrust it forward and pulled

Left: President William McKinley was assassinated by Leon Czolgosz.

Right: Leon Frank Czolgosz, assassin of President William McKinley.

the trigger twice. James "Big Jim" Parker, who was standing in line behind Czolgosz, acted quickly, punching the assassin in the neck and knocking him down. Czolgosz tried to fire the gun a third time, but Parker knocked it from his hand.

At first, the president seemed stunned. He rose to his toes and then took a step back before falling forward. Security guards began to beat Czolgosz, but McKinley ordered them to stop.

McKinley thought of his wife, Ida Saxon McKinley. "Be careful how you tell my wife," he said. Perhaps McKinley was thinking of how fragile she had become after suffering the deaths of their two daughters, her mother and grandfather all within a short period.

The assassin Czolgosz, one of eight children, was born in Detroit, Michigan, in 1873 to Polish immigrants. His first job at sixteen was near Pittsburgh at a glasswork. He earned seventy-five cents a day and saved his money to help his family move to Cleveland in 1891. His father operated a saloon at the corner of Tod Street (now 65th Street) and 3rd Avenue (now Gertrude Avenue). After a few years, the family moved to a farm in Warrensville Township.

When Czolgosz was eighteen, he found a job at the Newburgh Wire Mill in Cleveland. As he had only a sixth-grade education, the only work he was suited for was manual labor. He made $492 a year and remained employed year-round, but the working conditions at the mill were poor. After a few years, a price war put profits in a tailspin, so the company cut workers' meager wages. Czolgosz participated in a failed strike against the mill and was fired. He was blacklisted as a troublemaker. He managed to get his job back a year later by using the assumed name of Fred C. Nieman. Fred was a nickname his family called him, and Nieman meant "nobody." The whole episode made him bitter, and he began focusing on the economic disparity between the wealthy and the working classes.

Czolgosz read Edward Bellamy's *Looking Backward*, a novel about a time traveler who falls into a hypnotic sleep in the nineteenth century and awakens in the year 2000 to a socialist utopia. Czolgosz was so enthralled with the book that he reread it several times.

By 1898, Czolgosz had become mentally fragile and had a nervous breakdown. He quit his job and went to live with his devout Roman Catholic family on their farm. While there, he spent much of his time tinkering, fishing and rabbit hunting. He also read radical works. He became fascinated with Gaetano Bresci, the anarchist who in 1900 shot and killed Italy's King Umberto I because of his authoritarian regime. Czolgosz was so taken with Bresci that he collected newspaper clippings about the assassination.

Czolgosz was embittered further by his family's faith and returned to Cleveland in 1901. He had become aware of Emma Goldman, an anarchist who traveled the country speaking to crowded houses and selling her books and pamphlets. She railed against the Spanish-American War. Her lectures denounced the church, law and morality—all of which fit with Czolgosz's worldview.

Howard Dennis called Goldman "this high priestess of anarchy" in an article he wrote for *Modern Culture*, a magazine published in November 1901. He quoted part of her speech: "In no country save America is there a thinking man or woman who will admit a belief in the God of the Bible. The church has been succeeded by the law, but the law is as criminal as the church." Dennis wrote that he felt the intention was to inflame acts of violence.

Anarchist Emma Goldman.

Goldman spoke in Cleveland to full houses three times. One of those times was May 5, 1901, at Memorial Hall. She was sponsored by the Liberty Club, a group made up of radical thinkers. Several members of the Liberty Club came from the old Franklin Club, a local politically progressive group that embraced the ideas that "error is harmless if truth is free to combat it" and also "labor produces wealth."

Goldman lectured, "I do not approve of violence or assassination: but when it does take place, *the man who strikes the blow is a hero*. He has done what others who are suffering from oppression have not the courage to do."

Czolgosz was in the audience for this event, and her rhetoric resonated with him.

During the intermission, Czolgosz approached Goldman. Giving his name as Fred C. Nieman, he told her he was working in Cleveland and asked for a recommendation from the books and pamphlets that were for sale near the platform.

Goldman later described him as very young and of medium height with erect posture. "But it was his face that held me, a most sensitive face, with delicate pink complexion; a handsome face, made doubly so by his curly golden hair. Strength showed in his large blue eyes," she wrote in her autobiography, *Living My Life*.

After her lecture in Cleveland, she went to stay with the Isaak family in Chicago. Abraham Isaak was the editor of *Free Society*, an anarchist journal. Czolgosz turned up there to visit with her again. He told her he belonged to a socialist group in Cleveland but felt they lacked vision and enthusiasm. Czolgosz's enthusiasm, using terms like "comrade" and asking about "secret meetings," made Isaak suspicious of him. Isaak wondered if he was a clumsy spy. Czolgosz had attempted to join the Liberty Club in Cleveland, but he was refused membership. Isaak's Cleveland colleague Emil Schilling also thought he was a government spy. Another observer thought he was unstable and perhaps schizophrenic.

 That summer, Czolgosz read that President McKinley would visit the Pan-American Exposition and would give a speech there. On August 31, Czolgosz rented a room in the Polish section of Buffalo. On September 3, he bought a .32-caliber Iver Johnson pistol. Two days later, he was in the audience for McKinley's speech. The next day, September 6, he waited in the meet-and-greet line with the gun concealed in a handkerchief. McKinley was surrounded by bodyguards, but Czolgosz managed to walk up to the president and fire two bullets into him. He would have fired a third shot had it not been for James Parker.

Still conscious, McKinley was rushed to the Pan-American Exposition's hospital in an electric ambulance. Dr. Matthew Mann, dean of the University of Buffalo Medical School, was at the fair that day. Although he was a gynecological surgeon, he was the first physician to respond. McKinley was taken into surgery. According to Dr. Howard Markel, monthly columnist for the *PBS NewsHour*, Dr. Roswell Park, a surgeon with extensive experience in abdominal wounds, would have been a better choice, but he was in another surgery in Niagara Falls and would not leave that patient.

Dr. Mann put McKinley under with ether anesthesia. The doctor found the chest wound to be superficial, but the other bullet had passed through the president's stomach wall. The doctor sutured the holes but could not find the bullet itself, and he could not find any other bleeding, so he closed the wound in the president's abdomen. The president was given morphine for pain and a mixture of strychnine and brandy for heart stimulation.

At first, the president seemed to recover, but then on September 12, he took a turn for the worse. Dr. Charles Stockton, an internist and professor at the University of Buffalo Medical School, diagnosed McKinley with heart failure. President McKinley went downhill rapidly and died at 2:15 a.m. on September 14. An autopsy later showed gangrene had gone undetected on an internal wound. The bullet was never located.

On September 16, a funeral train transported the president's body, first to the United States Capitol in Washington, D.C., for a service and then home to Canton, Ohio.

Czolgosz confessed: "I killed President McKinley because I done my duty. I didn't believe one man should have so much service, and another man should have none."

He said Emma Goldman's speeches had influenced him. At first, authorities thought he was part of a conspiracy that included Goldman. She and others were briefly detained, but it was determined that Czolgosz had acted on his own.

Initially, the court assumed Czolgosz was insane, so he was examined by five doctors—three for the state and two for the defense—but he was found competent. He was tried by the Supreme Court of the State of New York. His trial was a short one. "I done my duty….I am an anarchist," he told the court. "I don't believe in the Republican form of government and I don't believe we should have any rulers. I had that idea when I shot the president and that is why I was there." From jury selection to the guilty verdict took two days.

Leon F. Czolgosz was sentenced to die in the electric chair. His execution took place on October 29, 1901. Unrepentant to the end, he said, "I am

President William McKinley and an unnamed man in a carriage on the day of his inauguration.

not sorry for my crime." He was dead within four minutes of the electricity entering his body. He was then buried in an unmarked grave on the prison grounds in Auburn, New York.

The McKinley Monument was dedicated on September 30, 1907. McKinley, Ida and their two daughters are entombed there. The monument, along with the McKinley Presidential Library and Museum, is at 800 McKinley Monument Drive, NW, in Canton.

Chapter 7

FRED KOHLER

Loved or Hated

Throughout Fred Kohler's careers as Cleveland police chief, Cleveland mayor and Cuyahoga County sheriff, he was either loved or hated. There was nothing in between. He was rude, arrogant and hard-nosed.

Kohler joined the Cleveland Police Department in 1880 when he was twenty-five. By 1900, he had clawed his way up to the rank of captain. As captain of his precinct, he was effective in reducing crime in the tenderloin district. He required a policeman to be stationed at the door of every bordello, drinking establishment and gambling house, and customers had to supply their names to the officer before they could enter. Rather than admit who they were, many patrons walked away. Kohler kept a "little black book" of those who gave their names. Vice resorts that broke any of the rules were raided and closed down.

Mayor Tom L. Johnson was told that the raids were an attempt on Kohler's part to embarrass the administration. The mayor's answer to that was to exile Kohler to a precinct at the outskirts of the city. Kohler did not complain or question the assignment. He put his head down and transformed that precinct. Under Kohler, patrolmen began to toe the line and look like professionals, making the precinct's population outwardly happy.

When Johnson saw the changes and heard of wide citizen approval, he decided he had made a mistake by banishing Kohler. Johnson hastened police chief George E. Corner's retirement and named Kohler to replace him.

Tom L. Johnson was Cleveland's mayor from 1901 to 1908.

In a year's time, Kohler had laid down the law to the police department and transformed it into a highly efficient organization. The officers were disciplined and smartly dressed. Patrolmen complained that he was too severe, but Kohler did not care whose spit-shined toes he stepped on.

Kohler instigated what he called the "sunrise court." It was a policy that called for hobos and tramps who had the bad luck to come into the city to be rounded up early every morning. Kohler's police then threw them into the back of a paddy wagon and drove them to the city limits, where they were dumped with a warning to not come back. Officials in the suburbs were vocally opposed to this. True to Kohler's nature, he did not care what the suburbs thought. East Cleveland police chief James Stanberger ordered his officers to wait at the city limits and round up the undesirables and cart them back into Cleveland. Stanberger finally got an injunction to get the practice stopped.

As far as liquor was concerned, Cleveland police were instructed to not charge intoxicated individuals the first time they were picked up. Instead,

President Theodore Roosevelt (*left*) with Cleveland police chief Fred Kohler.

they were taken home or locked up for the night. In the morning, they were made to sign waivers before they were let go. Offenders of low-level crimes, especially juveniles, were not arrested the first time they were caught. They were given a second chance. Kohler called this the "Golden Rule."

When President Teddy Roosevelt came to Cleveland in 1903 for the high-society wedding of Mark Hanna's daughter, Kohler had his troops turned out in crisp uniforms with gleaming buttons and polished shoes. Not one of them made a misstep. As for Kohler himself, he made sure he was always within the president's view. Roosevelt was so impressed with Kohler and his department that he told reporters, "You have the best chief of police in America in Kohler."

While Kohler may have won the president's praise, he had made a long list of enemies.

In 1909, Herman C. Baehr defeated Johnson for mayor. At last, Kohler's foes had a new mayor's ear. By May 1910, the anti-Kohler camp lodged several complaints of drunkenness and conduct unbecoming an officer against the chief. Whether they were true or not remained to be seen. Baehr announced twenty-one charges against Kohler and suspended him.

In typical Kohler style, he went on the attack and demanded to see the charges, but the mayor did not have them at his disposal. Kohler made sure this was made public. The Civil Service Commissioners, Samuel H.

Left: Herman C. Baehr was Cleveland's mayor from 1910 to 1912.

Right: Newton D. Baker Jr. served as Cleveland mayor from 1912 to 1915.

Holding, John T. Bourke and M.P. Rooney, held the hearing. After looking at the prosecution's evidence, the commissioners threw out ten of the twenty-one charges. Before the defense finished its presentation, the commission threw out eight more charges, leaving three to be dealt with.

Kohler's attorneys proved that the chief and his wife were at the opera house and not anywhere near where one of the alleged charges occurred. The other two charges were dispensed with when the law director, Newton D. Baker Jr., and former sheriff Edwin D. Barry testified against charges of drunkenness.

Kohler was exonerated, and Baehr had no choice but to reinstate him as police chief. Unfortunately, the chief would face the Civil Service Commission again three years later for a far more scandalous charge.

In the 1913 case, Kohler was accused of improper relations with a married woman. The peccadillo happened on June 5, 1912, when he was caught red-handed with Mae Connor Schearer by her husband, Samuel, in their home at 2606 Daisy Avenue, SW.

The *Cleveland Leader* covered the trial, which was held in the commission's chambers, a small room on the first floor of city hall. It accommodated only eighty-five people, leaving at least five hundred interested citizens out in the hallway. Commissioner Holding again sat in judgment, along with Ralph Edwards and William C. Keough.

Kohler was charged with neglect of duty and gross immorality. He claimed he was framed. Samuel D. Schearer told a different story.

Schearer was an ink salesman in charge of the Cleveland branch of the Charles Henry Johnson and Company Printing on St. Clair Avenue. He told the commissioners he left the house on the night in question around 7:00 p.m. on work errands. Apparently, he led his wife to believe he was going out of town. Instead, he came back to the duplex a couple of hours later.

Before going to his side of the house, he met his neighbor, Anna Merki, who owned and lived on the other side of the house. Charles A. Bull and Clayton P. Benjamin were also at Merki's. The men lingered about ten minutes before heading to the front porch on Schearer's side of the building. The house was dark, Schearer said. He rang the bell several times, but his wife did not answer it. He used his pocketknife to cut the screen so he could reach the latch and unfasten it, but the night lock was engaged on the inside door. He could not get in, so he and Bull tried using force with their shoulders. When that did not work, he tried to kick the door in. At that point, he said he heard someone inside calling, "Sam, Sam, he's getting out the back door." At that, he picked up a rocking chair and threw it through the front window.

Inside, he walked through the house, turning on lights. He claimed to have found Kohler crouching behind the refrigerator in a shed off the kitchen. According to Schearer, Kohler said, "I'm good; I'm bad. You've got me. What are you going to do with me?"

Schearer said Kohler's feet were bare. "I saw this through his shoes which were open, and I found Kohler's socks hanging out of his pockets."

The aggrieved husband then followed Kohler upstairs, where he found his wife clad in a robe, her hair hanging down her back. Schearer was so angry, he insisted that his wife pack her bags and leave.

Schearer divorced his wife a few months after the incident.

Anna Merki testified that she had seen Kohler visit Mae Schearer several times. She gave the dates of February 2 between 1:00 and 5:00 p.m., May 23 and June 5. On one occasion, she heard them in the kitchen. Another time, she watched them as they sat on the porch, and each time a car passed the house, Mae Schearer would get up and go in the house.

When asked how long she had known the Schearers, she said the couple had moved into another house she owned in 1903. Evidence showed the couple had married in July 1904.

To rebut Anna Merki's testimony, Kohler's defense attorney, William H. Boyd, called two doctors to testify. Dr. Maurice Budwig told the commissioners that on February 2, he made a house call at the Kohler residence, where the chief was in bed with a fever. He was coughing and had a sore throat. The doctor fixed that date by using his daybook and the prescription he had filled.

City solicitor E.K. Wilcox questioned Budwig about the appearance of the entry in the daybook. He said it looked as if it had been written over an erasure. The doctor said the entry had been rubbed, and there was no erasure.

The police surgeon, Dr. F.B. Norton, was next to testify. He said he had examined Kohler at the police station on January 3. He found he was sick and sent him home. Norton said the chief did not return to work until February 3.

On the day Kohler took the stand, he wore the same light gray suit, wing-collar shirt, light-colored tie and shiny black shoes he had worn on June 5 when he was caught at the Schearers' house. Sitting erect and trying not to show his natural arrogance, he testified for several hours.

He admitted being alone in the house with Mae Schearer, but he said they had known each other for several years and their friendship was innocent. He again claimed he was framed and said a woman had called him and asked for his personal protection. When Samuel Schearer came home, Kohler said he realized the woman who called was not Mae Schearer. He said it was a setup to entrap him, and he denied that he had been found with his clothing in "disarrangement" and that he had told Samuel Schearer that he was surrendering.

Kohler's defense was weak, and he was found guilty. He was discharged from office, and his pension was cut in half.

Kohler did not retreat in disgrace. Instead, he went to his favorite haunt, the Hollenden Hotel, the next night with his head held high, his posture challenging. He told the press, "All right, boys! I'll be leading the police department down Euclid Avenue again someday."

A month later, when he was on his way home from the Hollenden late one night, three thugs stepped out of the dark and beat him with brass knuckles and blackjacks and kicked him. He made it home on his own. Although he was laid up for a week with his injuries, he refused to get police involved.

Back on his feet, he began seeking a number of political offices. In 1913, he ran for city council but lost. The next year, he ran for county clerk and lost. He lost in 1915 when he ran for clerk of courts. In 1916, he lost his bid for sheriff. He waited to seek office again until 1918, when he ran for county councilman and won.

In that position, he set about to cause chaos, accusing the other two commissioners—who were Democrats, and he was a Republican—of being on the take. No county official who got in his way was safe from accusations.

In 1921, Kohler ran for mayor. During that campaign, he was asked if he thought women, who would be voting for the first time, would remember the Schearer scandal of 1913. He said they would vote for him. According to George E. Condon in *Cleveland: The Best Kept Secret*, Kohler said, "The women will remember two things about me. That I was a good police chief and kept the town clean, and that when I got into that mess, I protected the woman's name right from the start."

His campaign was simple. Relying on his reputation as police chief, he went door to door in every neighborhood and asked for votes. He also mailed out thousands of letters seeking votes. He brought in a public opinion poll expert from New York to find out what his odds were. Gamblers placed bets. One man bet several thousand dollars on Kohler, and it paid off. Kohler won.

During his inauguration day parade, he mounted a horse and led a police patrol down Euclid Avenue, making good on the promise he had made to reporters on the night he lost his job as police chief.

When Kohler took office, Cleveland was in deep financial peril. He set to work to put the city's economics in order. His first act was to fire 850 Republican ward workers and replace them with 200 of his handpicked people.

Within two years, the city went from having close to $2 million in deficit to a cash surplus of $1.8 million. He accomplished this by slashing the payroll and letting services and parks and other city properties become run-down.

In the spring of 1922, Kohler became inspired to paint the town orange and black.

Fred Kohler, fortieth mayor of Cleveland, from 1922 to 1924.

He hired painters to turn every city-owned building into his two favorite colors. When the papers asked him why he had ordered this paint job, he said, "Everybody can see all the buildings now that belong to the city, to the people. They can see them from a long way off.

"You can see them, can't you? Well, that's the big idea. I picked out the colors myself because orange and black are the most visible colors there are day or night."

In addition to the new color scheme, Kohler had huge billboards erected around the city. One at the east end of the Detroit-Superior high-level bridge read, "I kept the wolf from the door. FRED KOHLER, Mayor." Another one read, "Good or Bad. Right or Wrong. I Alone Have Been Your Mayor. FRED KOHLER, Mayor."

He kept up running battles with the utility companies, city council, Irish police and newspaper reporters. Maybe worst of all to sports fans, he outlawed prize fights.

In January 1924, the city manager plan of government took effect, replacing the mayoral-council form of city administration and putting Kohler out of office—but not for long. He took out petitions at the Board

Fred Kohler,
Cuyahoga County
sheriff.

of Elections to run for governor, county treasurer, coroner and county recorder. He settled on running for sheriff and had no problem winning that office.

Kohler was not sheriff for very long before his treatment of the prisoners at the jail was called into question. Although he was allotted forty-five cents a day for each prisoner's meals, he cut it down to seven cents a day. His critics claimed the balance—upward of $50,000—went into his pocket during his two-year term.

Voters denied him a second term in 1926.

In 1928, Kohler threw his hat into the ring for governor, but instead of campaigning, he toured Europe. Understandably, he was soundly defeated.

When the city manager form of government swung back to mayor-council form, Kohler gave every indication of running for mayor in 1930, but his political career was over. He was getting older, and his health was beginning to fail.

In 1932, he suffered a stroke while on board an ocean liner in the Plymouth, England harbor. A second stroke two years later ended his life.

After Kohler's death, the *Plain Dealer* reported that the county auditor found $34,500 in government bonds, $60,000 in Federal Farm Loan bonds and $60,500 in various savings accounts around the city. In addition, he owned Cleveland Railroad stock and a $25,000 certificate for paid up stock in the Mutual Building and Investment Company.

It was a mystery how a public servant amassed a half million dollars.

Chapter 8

"BIG JIM" MORTON, BANK ROBBER

*U*niformed policemen stood at the entrance of the old courthouse and scrutinized each person as he or she walked through the door. Up on the fifth floor, more police and deputy sheriffs guarded the entrance to Judge Frank C. Phillip's criminal courtroom. Security was tight for the James "Big Jim" Morton bank robbery trial that started on Tuesday, January 5, 1920. Sheriff Edward J. Henratty had foiled two escape attempts.

In addition to heavy law enforcement presence at the courthouse, six deputies surrounded Morton as they took him from the jail to the courthouse using the "bridge of sighs." The bridge stretched from the jail's fourth floor to the criminal courtroom on the fifth floor.

Morton, who was over six feet tall and weighed 188 pounds, was accused of leading the gang who robbed the West Cleveland Banking Company at Detroit Avenue, NW, and West 101ˢᵗ Street at 2:00 p.m. on June 16, 1919. Morton and three others got out the bank's door with more than $65,000.

Police captured Morton in Toledo. A second robber, Harry "Sheriff" Holmes, was also nabbed in Toledo, and a third, James "Tip" O'Neil, was arrested in Elyria. The fourth bandit, Herman "Harry" Diehm, was still on the loose. Morton denied knowing any of these men during his trial.

No amateur when it came to jail, Morton's first incarceration had been at the Pontiac, Illinois reformatory when he was seventeen. Later, he served prison terms at Folsom in California; Carson City, Nevada; and Salt Lake City, Utah.

The Cuyahoga County Courthouse where "Big Jim" Morton was tried and found guilty of bank robbery.

On the opening day of the trial, West Cleveland Banking Company's commercial teller Earl Stafford was the first witness for the prosecution. The Rocky River resident recalled the robbery for the jurors. He told them there were four cages in the bank, and he was in one of them. The other three were occupied by savings teller Lucille Shirkey and bookkeepers Elizabeth Jahneke and Emil Cotleur.

The *Plain Dealer* reported some of Stafford's testimony: "I was bending over, counting money when I heard a sharp command, 'Hold up your hands.' I looked up and saw a man covering me with a revolver." Three other men held guns on Shirkey, Jahneke and Cotleur as they walked around to the back of the cages, Stafford testified. The robber who held the gun on him ordered him to open the safe. Stafford told him three times he could not open the safe in the vault because he did not have the combination.

"If you don't open it, I'll blow out your brains," the big bandit said.

"I guess you'll have to blow out my brains then, because I don't know the combination."

At assistant county prosecutor Steven M. Young's bidding, Stafford pointed to Morton as the man who had threatened to kill him.

James Morton, Harry Holmes, James O'Neil and Harry Diehm robbed the West Cleveland Banking Company in 1919.

The teller continued to testify that after the employees were lined up against the back wall, three of the robbers helped themselves to the cash drawers. They also grabbed some bags of gold and shoved them into the bags with money from the tills, but they missed three sacks of gold. After cleaning out the cash drawers and vault of more than $65,000, the thieves locked Stafford and the other three employees in the vault and left.

Stafford told defense attorney Patrick J. Mulligan that he got a good look at the man who did the talking because he was standing directly in front of him, eight feet away. "He had a determined, set, cool look." Morton had sharp features, a ruddy complexion and strikingly pale blue eyes.

The next witness was Dr. John H. Brett. Brett's car had been stolen on June 10 (six days prior to the robbery) from a spot on Euclid Avenue and East 102nd Street. Police recovered the car the day after the stickup and surmised it had been used in the robbery.

Barton Mears was the next witness for the prosecution. As the owner of the Faultless Tire & Repair Company on Lorain Avenue at West 54th Street, he testified to installing a new battery in a car that was garaged behind the Franklin Apartments, 5601 Franklin Avenue, NW. He said he performed the work at James Morton's request a day or two before the robbery.

James Morton's defense attorney, Patrick J. Mulligan.

On day two of the trial, bank teller Lucille Shirkey came to the stand and told jurors that she saw three men advancing toward the cages with guns. She referred to them by their names, having learned who they were from police. Harry Holmes pointed a gun at her and told her to put her hands up. "Instead of doing so, I reached for a revolver which I had beneath the ledge in my cage." Holmes threatened to kill her if she reached for it again.

She testified that she saw a man at the front of the bank pointing a gun at Stafford. When Prosecutor Young asked her who that man was, she said it was Morton. Morton refuted that in a 1950 three-part series on his life of crime for the *Saturday Evening Post*. Although he admitted in the series that he was guilty of the robbery, he claimed, "She was wrong. I was the man who went behind the railing and directly to the vault."

Under questioning by defense attorney Mulligan, she said she had a good look at Morton because he was only ten to twelve feet away from her. "I had a three-quarters view of his face."

Mulligan asked if she became excited when the robber pointed his gun at her. She replied, "No. I wasn't excited and I wasn't afraid."

In order to place Morton in Cleveland, the prosecution called Anna R. Boehler of Columbus, who had been employed at the Franklin Apartments in the months before the robbery. She told the court that Morton had rented a suite there the last part of May before the robbery. In September, she had come back to Cleveland to view a police lineup, and she had picked out Morton as the tenant.

Katherine Fay testified that she had rented the suite to Morton on May 27 or 28 before the June 16 robbery. She described for the jury how the police had searched the suite a couple of days after the robbery and had taken several things with them. However, they had overlooked a newspaper-wrapped package that was under the sink.

When the prosecutor asked what was in the package, she replied, "Several bank books and various papers."

The prosecutor asked if there was any printing on the content. "Yes," she said. "One of the bank books had the name West Cleveland Banking

Company on it." She told the jury she had not seen Morton after the robbery until she identified him from a lineup at police headquarters.

Attorney Mulligan questioned her about seeing police photos of Morton and then seeing him in the lineup. She had not recognized him from the photos, but she did recognize him in the lineup. Mulligan asked her what she said when she identified Morton. She did not remember her exact words.

"Didn't he say to you, 'You are mistaken'?"

"I don't remember that he said anything."

Cleveland police captain George Matowitz testified that during the search of the suite, he found a black travel bag and an old straw hat. He said Mrs. Fay had given him the papers and travelers' checks from the package found under the sink. Young showed him the papers and checks. He identified them, and they were entered into evidence.

Bank secretary Howard H. Butler identified the checks as belonging to the West Cleveland Banking Company. He also recognized one of the bank books that was in the vault on the morning of the robbery.

During his opening statement, Young had told the jury that the getaway car bore Michigan plates. During the prosecution's case, he called Cleveland police detective captain Harry Brown, who testified to finding Ohio and Michigan license plates in the Franklin suite during the search.

Morton took the stand in his own defense. "I was in Chicago at the time the robbery was committed," he said. "I was in Chicago on June 15 and 16." He claimed he was at various places, staying in the Florence hotel and visiting another on the fifteenth. He named several people he had met and talked with on those particular dates. He said he had lunch with a friend at the North American Café on the sixteenth and then went to a gambling house that evening.

After that, he said he went to Toledo. From there, he traveled to New York "and other places" before returning to Toledo. He was arrested in Toledo on August 31.

Under questioning from the prosecution, Morton denied he had ever been in Cleveland before police brought him to the city. He testified about his experience of being in a police lineup. He was in the middle of the line at first, but he changed his place to near the end. He said Stafford looked over the men but said nothing, so police told the men in the lineup to walk around the room. After police ordered the line to stop, Stafford picked him out.

Morton testified to being in a number of other lineups where Katherine Fay and Anna Boehler recognized him as the man who rented a suite in the

Franklin Apartments before the robbery. Police also took him to the bank, where Lucille Shirkey identified him.

Prosecutor Young asked Morton if he had recently sent a letter from jail to Mrs. Mabel Beman of Chicago, asking her to find out where he was on the dates in question. Morton admitted that he had written to her but denied sending a sample of his signature so someone could forge it on the Florence hotel registry, as Young accused.

Young asked Morton about his criminal record. "When were you released from the Illinois State Reformatory?"

"I wasn't released. I escaped." He was still wanted for that escape.

The question and answer were struck, but his aliases were brought out by the prosecutor. Morton said his real name was James Franklin, but the police knew he used various names, including James Morton, Magnus Olsen, James Farmer, Frank Z. Wilson and Joe Murray. William M. Alder, author of *The Man Who Never Died: The Life, Times, and Legacy of Joe Hill, American Labor Icon*, tracked Morton through historical newspapers, police and prison records and other documents and believes he was really Magnus Olsen, a violent criminal.

Defense attorney Mulligan argued that his client could not get a free and public trial. He said people were indiscriminately barred from the trial and that the jury was intimidated by the heavy police presence. Judge Phillips

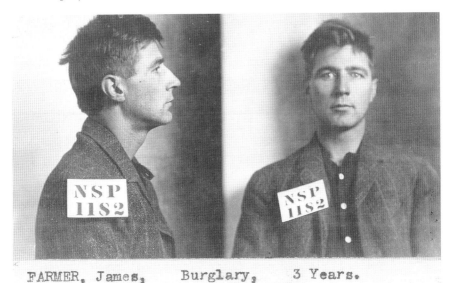

FARMER, James, Burglary, 3 Years.

Magnus Olsen, aka James Farmer, aka James Morton, mug shots, Nevada State Penitentiary, 1908. *Nevada State Library and Archives.*

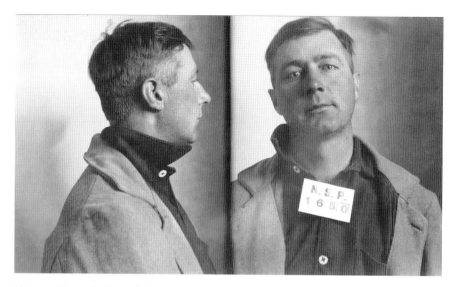

Magnus Olsen, aka James Morton, mug shots, Nevada State Penitentiary, 1914. *Nevada State Library and Archives*.

said he had instructed the sheriff to take precautionary measure because Morton's associates had attempted to break him out of jail twice.

During his closing argument, Mulligan said that even before the trial began, there was a "systematic attempt" to create the impression that Morton was the ringleader of a gang of thieves. He asserted that the extreme police presence was an "unfair method" to impress the jury. "It was all a part of the drama of the scene, which was acted before your eyes."

He told the jury that Morton had tried to get depositions from the people who had seen and talked with him in Chicago on the date of the robbery, "but the Ohio constitution forbids the taking of depositions outside the state in a case where the defendant is in jail."

Mulligan did his best to defend Morton, pointing out weaknesses in each of the state's witnesses and inconsistencies in the prosecution's case. Lastly, he told the jury that Morton was on trial simply because of his criminal record.

Jurors began deliberating after lunch on Thursday, January 8. By 9:30 p.m., they returned a sealed verdict of guilty. Mulligan polled the jury, but it did not matter. His client was going to jail.

Morton was sentenced to an indeterminate term of one to fifteen years. "If the board of paroles at Columbus lets you out before the end of fifteen years, the people who know of your crime will be justified in feeling contempt for that board," Judge Phillips said.

Morton showed no emotion at the verdict or sentence.

Although the law provided for only one guard per prisoner bound for the state penitentiary, the Common Pleas Criminal Journal showed that Judge Phillips ordered four guards to accompany Morton to the Ohio State Penitentiary.

Mulligan filed a petition for a new trial. During the next two years, the attorney sought a pardon for Morton from Governor Harry L. Davis, as well as a parole. Both were denied. Prosecutor Young said he considered Morton "the most dangerous criminal ever convicted in Cuyahoga County."

Morton lived up to Young's description while at the penitentiary. He committed several infractions for lying and "disobedience of orders and inattention." Prison officials segregated him from the other prisoners. They said he was hopeless and should be guarded carefully.

Near the end of November 1922, Morton was granted a new trial by a four-to-three vote of the Ohio Supreme Court. The justices found that he had not been allowed to depose witnesses in Chicago. A new prosecutor, Edward C. Stanton, was adamant that Morton not be allowed to travel to secure depositions. Bail was set for $100,000, a sum Morton was unable to raise, so he remained in prison until the second trial, when he was convicted again.

On April 21, 1930, a fire broke out in the penitentiary. Started by an oily rag that came in contact with a lighted candle, the blaze ripped through the prison, killing 322 prisoners and hospitalizing 230. Morton became a hero when he dragged 20 men to safety and then collapsed from smoke inhalation. He won parole after that.

James Morton may have been a hero during the prison fire, but records showed him to be a consummate liar, a dangerous and violent criminal. According to Adler, Morton used many different names, falsified countless records and committed crimes in almost every state. He was a robber, a burglar, a safecracker, an arsonist and most likely a murderer.

Adler argued in his book that Morton, who was going by the name Frank Z. Wilson in 1914, murdered Salt Lake City grocer John G. Morrison and his two young sons during a robbery. Labor troubadour and activist for the Industrial Workers of the World Joe Hill—who looked very much like Morton/Wilson—was convicted on ambiguous evidence and executed by firing squad for the deaths. Hill was later immortalized in the ballad "Joe Hill," written by Alfred Hayes and Earl Robinson and performed by Joan Baez at Woodstock.

Morton admitted to being "part-time on Al Capone's payroll" in the 1950 three-part serial published in the *Saturday Evening Post*. He claimed to be a "collector" and "bodyguard" for Capone and said that Capone had "connections" when it came to getting someone out of jail. But Adler writes that while going under the name Wilson, Morton most certainly took part in the St. Valentine's Day Massacre, and he owned the murderers' getaway car.

In the *Saturday Evening Post* series, Morton smugly said, "I was a smart thief, too, as smart as they come. The cops still haven't caught up with me on most of the jobs I pulled."

Chapter 9

COP KILLER

*O*n May 14, 1923, the naked body of Cleveland patrolman Dennis Griffin was found in a shallow grave at the base of an uprooted tree near Pettibone Road in Bainbridge Township in Geauga County. Pieces of his charred uniform and the shovel used to dig the grave were recovered two hundred feet away. The thirty-nine-year-old father of a nine-month-old baby had been shot in the neck, and there was a deep gash over his left eye.

Hundreds of police and volunteers had searched for Griffin since he went missing after he arrested John Leonard Whitfield on May 11.

On the night of May 10 going into the morning of May 11, Patrolman Harry T. Hughes was stationed at Whitfield's garage behind his Elgin Avenue house. Whitfield dealt in spark plugs, and police suspected many of them were stolen. Hughes was waiting for Whitfield to come home so he could arrest him for receiving stolen property. Griffin was due to relieve Hughes at 6:00 a.m.

Just before Griffin arrived, Whitfield drove into the garage. When Hughes placed him under arrest, Whitfield pulled out a fat roll of bills from his pocket and offered a bribe. "Of course, I told him 'nothing doing' on the money stuff, and that he'd have to come along with me," Hughes told the *Plain Dealer*.

Once Griffin came on the scene, he and Hughes searched Whitfield and got ready to take him to the station. Before they left, Whitfield asked to speak to his wife about bail money. Griffin and Hughes followed Whitfield into the

Left: Cleveland patrolman Dennis Griffin was killed by John Leonard Whitfield.

Right: Cleveland patrolman Harry T. Hughes was the last person to see Dennis Griffin alive. *Krueger Studios, Cleveland Public Library.*

two-story house. Mary Whitfield was clad in a thin nightgown and quickly disappeared into the upstairs bedroom. Wanting to give the woman privacy, the two policemen allowed Whitfield to follow her into the bedroom while they waited in the hall. Moments later, Whitfield came out of the bedroom. Unbelievably, Griffin and Hughes allowed Whitfield to follow them down the stairs and out to the curb.

"Griffin couldn't drive," Hughes told the papers. "So I said I would drive the extra car (Whitfield had two automobiles) and Griffin could let the prisoner drive the other car. And ride with him." Hughes was referring to the two 1917 Jordan roadsters owned by Whitfield.

Griffin left in the passenger seat with the prisoner driving one of the cars. Hughes followed, driving the other Jordan. As Hughes was leaving the yard, he drove over the curb, causing the tires to lose air. "I called to Griffin and the prisoner not to go so fast because with low tires I couldn't keep up.

"But they kept going faster and faster and before I got to St. Clair Avenue (and Parkwood Drive), they had disappeared entirely. I was unable to see what direction they took. I learned of the escape of course when I got to the station."

When questioned, Mary Whitfield told police her husband had slipped a .45-caliber revolver into his pocket when he came into the bedroom. Captain George Matowitz, who would later become the Cleveland police chief, ordered an all-out search for Patrolman Griffin. At first, police hoped to find him alive, but as time passed, and with the knowledge that Whitfield was armed, hope faded.

Inspector Stephen Murphy directed the search. He shared a theory with the *Plain Dealer*: "When the prisoner went to get the gun, he was determined he would never allow himself to be taken to the precinct station." He went on to say that most gunmen try to ditch their weapons upon arrest, as a concealed weapon charge carries a stiff sentence.

It did not take long for police to realize they needed the public's help. They went to the press and the radio stations in hopes the publicity would bring in tips and sightings, particularly by farmers who lived along roads that led out of Cleveland. The reports gave out Whitfield's description as being dark skinned, possibly Mexican or Black. He wore a Charlie Chaplin–style moustache and was about forty years old, five feet, ten inches tall with a "stocky, fleshy appearance," weighing maybe two hundred pounds. His car was one of only two of a kind—a Jordan built in 1917. It had a blue body, a nickel-plated radiator and red wheels. It carried two spare wheels in the rear.

By evening, tips started to flow in. East Cleveland resident George Dixon saw the car speeding past his home. A policeman was huddled in the passenger seat, he said. "My attention was attracted to the car by a report that sounded like a blowout. I am now convinced it was a shot." He told police the driver pushed the policeman down in the seat. At first, it looked to Dixon like the policeman was drunk.

On Sunday, May 13, another person came forward to tell police he had spotted a car with a man driving it that answered Whitfield's description. He had seen it along Pettibone Road between Geauga Lake and Bainbridge, so searchers began to concentrate in that area.

Next, three boys found the remains of a fire on Pettibone's roadway. Charred fragments of a policeman's coat, shoes, nightstick and two brass buttons bearing the number 14 (14th Police Precinct, Griffin's precinct) were

John Leonard Whitfield.

John Whitfield's sport touring car.

among the ashes. As detectives sifted through the cinders, they found part of a holster, a belt buckle and a pointed-blade shovel with an extra bolt attached. More tips poured in, including one from a woman named Agnes Briel. She said that on Friday—the morning Griffin disappeared—she lent a shovel to a man who answered Whitfield's description.

Police and volunteers started to focus their search for Griffin in the area of Pettibone Road. They found two places where Whitfield had possibly tried to dig a grave, but the soil was too rocky.

Griffin's grave was finally located two hundred feet from the scorched remains of his clothing. Police figured Whitfield had stripped Griffin so if his body was ever found, it would be harder to identify him. But the murderer had made a mistake by burning the clothing in the middle of the road where the fire was so easily found. If he had set the clothing on fire in the woods, it might never have been found, and neither would the body.

They then concentrated on finding John Leonard Whitfield. It was a countywide search that quickly became a statewide and then several-states-wide manhunt.

As the police investigated Whitfield's background, they found he was leading a double life. Mary Whitfield was his legal wife. She explained that she had seen little of her husband in the preceding weeks. "He was too busy with business of which I knew nothing. He came home early in the morning and usually left after dark. He told me he was in the garage business." She knew something was wrong and learned he was seeing a very young girl who lived on East 93rd. Her name was Marie Agnes Price. Marie called herself Mrs. Whitfield. She was fourteen years old and pregnant. The girl had met Whitfield when he came to her school.

Surprisingly, Whitfield's wife invited Marie to come live with them because she felt sorry for the girl. She even bought Marie a hat and shoes and made her a dress. After a while, Marie became disrespectful and told Mary Whitfield that "she could break up my home any time she wanted to." After that, Whitfield took Marie away.

In the hours after he killed Griffin, Whitfield doubled back to Cleveland to get money out of the bank and pick up Marie. By this time, law enforcement from every city and state was on the lookout for him. They tracked the fugitive and his young girlfriend through Ohio, Indiana, Illinois and into Wisconsin by police reports and the public's tips until the couple stopped at Chili Al's, a restaurant in Madison. Chili Al's proprietor recognized Whitfield and sent a waiter to get the police. In the meantime, he slowed their food order to give officers time to arrive.

When two Madison cops showed up, one of them went in the front entrance while the other went in the back door. One drew his gun and aimed it at Whitfield. The fugitive made no resistance, so the two officers walked him out of the restaurant (unbelievably again) without handcuffs. As they walked to the patrol car, Whitfield suddenly jerked away and ran up an alleyway. One of the patrolmen emptied his pistol at Whitfield and thought the fugitive staggered a bit but kept running.

During the fracas, Marie had walked out of the restaurant and down the street. Officers spotted her and picked her up. She claimed to be deeply in love with Whitfield and was most happy to talk about him and their trip.

Griffin's murder was news to her. Whitfield had told her he gave the patrolman $100 as a bribe and dropped him at the station. She told them he had changed the looks of the car, and she had wondered why he did that. After leaving Cleveland, they made many stops along the way so he could sell spark plugs.

Whitfield had led Marie to believe they were going to get married and this trip was part of their honeymoon. Her baby was due in two months, so they had brought clothing and supplies for the child.

After Whitfield's Madison escape, he stole a 1920 green Buick touring car and got on the road. By evening, police were certain he had left Madison.

Mrs. Orabelle Price (*left*), mother of Marie Price (*right*), Whitfield's pregnant girlfriend. *N.B. Ruud, Cleveland Public Library.*

Again, authorities followed tips and sightings that came in from West Virginia to Pennsylvania to New York and Massachusetts. The best information came from Dewey Biggs, who said Whitfield had stopped at his garage in Chicago and tried to sell him a stolen Buick. Whitfield gave him a revolver, and police were certain it was the gun used to kill Griffin.

On June 26, the ten-week nationwide manhunt for cop killer John Leonard Whitfield finally ended in Detroit. On a solid tip from a bookkeeper for the Ternes Coal and Lumber Company, Cleveland police lieutenant Charles O. Nevel and detective Edward Conroy drove to the Michigan city. There, they enlisted the help of twenty-five Detroit policemen to surround the company on Michigan Avenue where Whitfield had been working for six weeks under the name Sam De Cario. Told to shoot at any suspicious move, the posse lay in wait for Whitfield to come out of the building.

At last, he came out into the yard and started to walk toward the office. When he saw five men approaching him, he quickened his pace. Police closed in on him, guns drawn. He acknowledged who he was and gave no resistance. This time, police snapped the cuffs on him.

Whitfield waived extradition and was brought back to Ohio. To avoid the crowds that such a high-profile case might draw, Chief Jacob Graul had Nevel and Conroy take him off the train in Elyria before getting to Union Depot. Graul, Nevel and Conroy were supposedly the only three people who knew of the Elyria location, so they were surprised when the train was met by a crowd of at least five hundred people. At first, Whitfield tried to smile when he saw all the gawkers, but he could not hold the smile for long. As police moved him through the crowd, he became stoic, looking down or straight ahead.

By comparison, several thousand people were waiting at the Cleveland depot to get a look at the cop killer who had dominated the front pages of the papers. When they learned he had been taken off the train in Elyria, they were greatly disappointed.

Under interrogation at the police station, Whitfield refused to say much about Griffin. He claimed he had been willing to go along with Griffin to the station on the morning of May 11, but Patrolman Griffin had stuck a gun in his side. "No matter how willing you are to submit to arrest, nobody wants to have a gun shoved in his ribs," he told police. "I struck the gun upward and it went off. It hit Griffin in the neck. He was hurt but not seriously, so I let him out at the police station to find a doctor."

Whitfield swore he did not know Griffin was dead, and he further swore he knew nothing about burying him. When he was confronted with the

Whitfield's jury found him guilty and recommended life in prison.

Agnes Briel statement about the shovel, he insisted she was "crazy!" But when faced with Mrs. Briel, he changed his story and declared he borrowed the shovel for another man, and it was the other man who buried Griffin; he stuck to the story of Griffin shooting himself during the struggle.

Mary Whitfield hired former state senator Arthur H. Day, former assistant prosecutor Blasé A. Buonpane and Alfred DeLorenzo to defend her husband. James T. Cassidy prosecuted the case for Cuyahoga County. At trial, he gave a dramatic opening statement. In part, he said, "If the ghastly form of Dennis Griffin—the victim of the most cold-blooded and brutal murder in the county or any other county—were to stalk into this courtroom, it would point an accusing finger at John L. Whitfield."

Whitfield took the stand in his own defense, but the three women and nine men of the jury were not swayed by his version of what happened. They found him guilty, and in spite of Cassidy asking for the death penalty, they recommended life imprisonment, which astounded Judge Frank C. Phillips.

Whitfield's story might have ended with a life sentence in the Ohio State Penitentiary except for his scaling the prison walls using a rope of mattress ticking at 2:00 a.m. on March 10, 1928. He had succeeded in smooth-talking one of the guards, Oren Hill, into helping him with the escape. He promised Hill, the father of five small children, a farm and $2,000 to $3,000 in cash if he would leave unbarred the iron door of the dormitory where Whitfield slept. Hill, a former brakeman for the railroad, was skeptical, but he was new at his job and had not had a paycheck in more than three months. "It looked like easy money and a chance to get a start. I had been out of work for a long time."

Warden Thomas found out Hill was involved and questioned him. The guard admitted his part in the escape. On a hunch, Thomas sent police to Hill's house. His hunch paid off. Hill's wife had provided a place for Whitfield to stay in the family home. He was cornered there by a Columbus detective and a parole officer. Whitfield was mortally wounded by a pump gun during a desperate attempt to run. He died that night.

Chapter 10

"FAST EDDIE" WATKINS

On Wednesday, October 29, 1975, Edward Owen Watkins strolled into the Society National Bank at 13681 Lorain Avenue. The fifty-six-year-old looked like any other customer. He was wearing a brown and green stingy-brim hat and heavy-framed glasses and was carrying a briefcase. But he was not there to cash a paycheck or make a deposit. He was there to withdraw the bank's entire assets.

"Fast Eddie," as he became known for his ability to rob and get in and out of a bank quickly, had knocked over fifty-four or fifty-five other banks from California to Cleveland, but the Society National Bank was special. It would prove to the newspapers, police and the bank that he still had what it took to relieve the institution of its money. He was not young anymore, but he could still live up to his legendary name.

Just months out of the Atlanta Federal Penitentiary, Eddie had broken parole and robbed a couple of banks in California. A heart attack slowed him down at the end of September. Two weeks later, he had a second attack. He was hospitalized on both occasions. When he felt better, he left the second hospital against doctor's orders. Near the end of October, he was back in Cleveland for a nostalgic tour of his younger years.

In their 1983 book *Fast Eddie*, Neil F. Bayne and Wes Sarginson wrote that Eddie picked up a Cleveland newspaper one day with an article that mentioned him. The article quoted the head of the Cleveland police robbery squad, Lieutenant Stanley J. Deka, who said robbers of the past like "Fast Eddie" Watkins could not get away with robbing a bank in 1970s

Cleveland because of new procedures. An ad for Society National Bank appeared on the next page, claiming the bank was so secure not even "Fast Eddie" Watkins would try to rob it.

The article and ad were a challenge to Eddie. He cased the bank to see how many employees worked there and found out the manager's name. It looked good, so he decided to hit it. His heart attacks had forced him to lay off cigarettes and liquor but not give up bank robbery.

He made a fake bomb out of a shoebox and masking tape. A transistor radio made it look realistic. He put it and a loaded .357 magnum into a briefcase and set off for the bank.

He parked his Buick down the street from the bank at Lorain and West 137th and walked into the bank around 2:30 p.m. A young woman greeted him. He asked to talk to William S. Hann, the manager, but was told Mr. Hann was busy with other customers. Eddie glanced over at Hann's desk and saw the manager was talking with a couple. Eddie returned his attention to the young woman and told her he would wait. After a short time, the couple at Hann's desk stood up, shook hands with Hann and left.

Hann looked over at Eddie, smiled and motioned him to his desk. Eddie took the chair Hann indicated and placed the fake bomb on the desk. He set his briefcase containing the loaded gun on the floor. Then he slid a letter out of his pocket and handed it to Hann.

According to *Fast Eddie*, the letter read: "This is a holdup. Sitting on your desk is a

Top: Young bank robber "Fast Eddie" Watkins. ©*1937, the* Plain Dealer. *All rights reserved. Reprinted/used with permission.*

Bottom: Lieutenant Stanley J. Deka, head of Cleveland robbery squad. *Photo by Horton, Cleveland Public Library.*

box of dynamite and in my hand is an electronically controlled plunger. One wrong move and you are dead. Smile if you intend to cooperate."

Eddie instructed Hann to gather everyone in the bank (seven cashiers and one customer) to the middle of the lobby. He ordered Hann to clear the vault of the money and put it in the briefcase. Hann explained he could not do that, as the vault was on a time lock and would not open for a few more minutes. Eddie had not been counting on this, but he said he would wait. As the minutes ticked by, he kept the fake bomb and .357 in full view. According to Bayne and Sarginson, the vault opened on time, and Eddie began stuffing the money—estimated at $100,000—into his briefcase.

The authors wrote that Eddie thought everything was going as planned, until he started to feel a familiar tightness and sharp pain in his chest. He knew what that meant. He reached in his pocket for his Peritrate Nitro and codeine tablets, but he had left them in his car. The pains subsided after a bit.

Without Eddie knowing, someone or something had triggered the silent alarm, alerting the police. Two patrolmen, Robert Taski and Robert Edmonds, were close by and responded within minutes. They managed to slip into the bank without Eddie seeing or hearing them. They observed an as-yet-identified robber stashing money from the cashiers' drawers into a briefcase. And they saw his gun. Taski pointed a shotgun at him. "Drop it."

Eddie might have been startled, but he quickly held up the fake bomb. In all of the bank jobs he had pulled, he had never resorted to violence. But this was different. This time, he was desperate. He was so close to getting away.

Taski later told *Plain Dealer* reporters Donald L. Bean and Robert J. McAuley that the robber said, "If you shoot, we're all going to die together. I haven't anything to lose." At that, Taski lowered the shotgun, and he and Edmonds slowly backed out the door and radioed for assistance.

Eddie knew it was only a matter of minutes before the bank would be surrounded by cops. He herded the eight hostages into a back room, which served as an employee lounge/lunchroom, and barricaded the door with chairs. He instructed two of the women to sit on the chairs.

Eddie was right. Cleveland police and an FBI strategy team quickly responded and took up positions. Special Agent J. Bernard "Bernie" Thompson was one of them. Sally Domm wrote in her article "With Death You Talk Softly" for the *Plain Dealer* that twelve-year veteran Thompson had just completed two weeks of hostage negotiation training. Only eleven minutes after the alarm went off, Thompson walked into the bank, picked up the intercom and learned who he was dealing with. It was a first for

"Fast Eddie" Watkins during the robbery of Society National Bank. © *1975, the* Plain Dealer. *All rights reserved. Reprinted/used with permission.*

both men—Thompson's first hostage situation and Eddie's first time taking hostages.

The standoff went on throughout the rest of the day, all night and into the next day. The book *Fast Eddie* and newspaper accounts differ in the chronology of the event. Both agree that Thompson kept talking to the bank robber, always urging him to give up and let the hostages go. Eddie steadfastly refused, but over the hours, he released one man and four women—all who either needed their medications or needed medical attention. Between 3:00 p.m. and 3:30 p.m., he released two of the women.

Bayne and Sarginson described the situation from Eddie's standpoint. He was afraid that if he surrendered, he would never get out of jail again. He insisted he was not going back to prison under any circumstances and kept reminding Thompson that he had a bomb and would blow everyone up.

Before the first hour was up, 160 police, FBI and sharpshooters swarmed the area. Fire trucks, police cruisers and ambulances lined the street. Police rerouted traffic and kept a gathering crowd across the street. Northeast Ohio's public were watching the drama unfold on television and hearing it on the radio. Over the years, Eddie had drawn "fans." When it became public who the robber was, his supporters started calling the bank and talking to him, even offering to harbor him or to lend him their cars.

After a few hours, Eddie's chest pains returned. He needed to get out of the bank, and he needed to get his medicine. At 4:00 p.m., he got on the phone with Thompson and laid out the demand for a van and $100,000. He thought he could drive the van to a spot where he had stashed a second car and then leave the van and disappear in his own car with one of the female hostages. It was reported he also asked for a plane and pilot.

Thompson relented. A half hour later, a white van drove up to the front of the bank just as Eddie requested. But the FBI had no intentions of letting him drive away. A mechanic had drained the oil from the crank case, so it could not go far, and the roof had been marked so helicopters could identify it. One of Eddie's outside supporters found out the van was rigged and called him on the phone to warn him. The FBI intercepted the call and had Ohio Bell disconnect the incoming line after that. The intercom remained open so the FBI could talk to Eddie.

The bomb was the biggest worry to law enforcement. At 5:00 p.m., they called out a bomb-sniffing dog and handler. By this time, police had determined the Buick parked on Lorain belonged to Eddie. The dog sniffed the car but did not react, so the handler took the dog to the door of the room where Eddie was holding the hostages. Again, the animal did not react. Police and FBI then thought Eddie might be bluffing. Knowing he had a gun, they still remained cautious.

The strategy team ordered the heat turned up inside the room where Eddie held the hostages. The temperature became almost unbearable. The electricity was also turned off. The room had a stove, refrigerator and coffee pot, so up until that time, Eddie and the hostages had been able to fix coffee and some food for themselves.

After a while, Eddie and the hostages had smoked all their combined cigarettes, so the robber demanded smokes, his favorite Pall Malls. Thompson sent the cigarettes in, and Eddie shared them with the hostages. As the hours stretched out, the hostages had begun to identify with Eddie, and they were concerned with his condition. His pains were coming in waves, and he was short of breath.

In the evening, Thompson, police chief Floyd F. Garey and Lieutenant Deka dug up some of Eddie's old friends, including his ex-wife, Karen, and a couple of old cellmates, in hopes they could persuade him to surrender. None of them swayed Eddie.

Around 7:00 p.m., United States district judge William K. Thomas came into the bank and talked to Eddie over the intercom. Judge Thomas had sentenced Eddie in 1965 to forty-seven years in prison for a string of fourteen robberies, but the two had forged an unlikely friendship. Eddie was a talented artist, and the judge even had some of Eddie's paintings hanging on his office walls. Most importantly, Eddie trusted him.

Eddie told the judge about his heart attacks in California and admitted that he was currently having pains. He told the judge his medicine was in his car and asked him to get it. Thomas retrieved the medication and slid it under the door to him.

The two talked for a while. Eddie told the judge about his time in prison. He spoke of the horrible conditions he had lived under and the terrible treatment he had received. He told the judge he was determined to not spend another day in jail. According to Bayne and Sarginson's book, Eddie told the judge, "You and I have always gotten along fine, but I'm through with jails. I'm making my last stand here. All the FBI can do is kill me, and that's not as bad as prison."

At 9:45 p.m., another one of the hostages became ill, and Eddie released her. Judge Thomas stayed in the bank negotiating with Eddie until 10:00 p.m.

It had been hours since Eddie and the hostages had eaten. Finally, around 2:00 a.m., the tactical team sent in hamburgers that were close to inedible. At that time, they found the hostages were calm and were even joking with Eddie.

By 5:00 a.m., Eddie's left arm was numb and he was dizzy. His speech was becoming inconsistent. Special Agent Thompson and Judge Thomas could tell he was fading.

Between 11:00 and 11:30 a.m., Eddie released two more hostages—one of them the manager—and asked for more medication. When Thompson came to the door with the medication, Eddie asked for an hour to decide if he should surrender. Fifteen minutes later, he released the rest of the hostages. They were reluctant to leave him. One of them hugged him.

Minutes later, he wanted to talk to Thompson face to face. Thompson told freelance writer Sally Domm that he was tired after the ordeal but felt confident when he walked into the room with Eddie. "I guess my guard was down," he told her. Eddie was propped against the wall with his .357 magnum within reach. Eddie picked up the gun.

"There I was, right in front of him," Thompson said. "I knew there was nothing in the world I could do and that if he wanted to pull the trigger, it was going to be over."

"Fast Eddie" Watkins in chains. He robbed fifty-five banks in his career. © *1967, Richard Misch/the* Plain Dealer. *All rights reserved. Reprinted/used with permission.*

He told Eddie that there was an ambulance waiting for him. Eddie lowered the gun. Judge Thomas came into the room, and the two men helped "Fast Eddie" out of the bank at 11:50 a.m. The 21½-hour standoff was over.

Eddie Watkins had spent more than thirty of his fifty-six years in prison and claimed to have robbed banks of $1.5 million. He buried $100,000 of it near Albuquerque, New Mexico. When he went back to retrieve it, he found a highway had been built over the spot.

He survived the heart attack he suffered during the Society National Bank robbery/hostage situation and was sent back to maximum-security prison in Atlanta. The courts and law enforcement thought he would never see the light of day again. But while he was in prison, "Fast Eddie" came up with a new plan. He was not done with Cleveland.

....

PART III

BLAZES, BOMBS AND BEER

Chapter 11

THE BURNING RIVER

A spark can be a good thing or a bad thing. It can be the dawn of something new and exciting, or it can be the catalyst for a calamity.

In the case of the Sunday, June 22, 1969 Cuyahoga River fire, it is believed that a spark thrown from a passing railcar ignited the oil on the polluted river's surface. The fire did $50,000 worth of damage to two railroad trestles. The blaze started around noon. Using a fireboat and other fire equipment, land-based firefighters had it extinguished within twenty-four minutes. Fires on the river had become such a common occurrence that few photos are known to exist, and the story warranted only a brief mention in the newspapers at the time. While the 1969 fire had the most notoriety, the Cuyahoga River had burned at least ten times within a one-hundred-year period.

Before the fires, and before the industrial pollution that caused the fires, the Cuyahoga River sustained life. It teemed with fish and other aquatic animals and plants. It quenched the thirst of beaver, muskrats, otters and deer. Nearby trees held eagles' nests. The river was important to the Native Americans for food. They called it Ka-ih-ogh-ha, meaning "crooked," and used it for thousands of years for travel and trade routes.

By the 1600s, explorers and surveyors had located the river. It appeared on maps after that and brought fur traders who built trading posts. More settlers came in the 1700s. Slowly, the Indians and much of the wildlife were displaced. On July 22, 1796, Moses Cleaveland arrived at the mouth of the river where it flowed into Lake Erie. On behalf of the Connecticut

Cleveland firefighters hose down a charred railroad trestle after a fire on the Cuyahoga River. *Photo by Michael J. Zaremba, Cleveland Public Library.*

Land Company, he put his surveyors to work plotting out the capital of the Western Reserve. The area had so much to offer that it grew into the city of Cleveland.

By the early 1800s, it was a challenge to move goods in and out of the area. The river itself was not suitable for transportation. Visionaries decided the water would be useful to fill a canal that could be built alongside the river and connect to other canals. After two years of work, the Ohio & Erie Canal opened in 1827. It was a transportation highway, using the river's water.

After the Civil War, manufacturing came to the banks of the Cuyahoga. Winding through Cleveland, the river became the perfect place for iron and steel mills. Paint companies set up shop. Warehouses for storing goods stood along the shore. It was a good place for shipyards to build and dock boats that would transport goods to the rest of the world. Before long, big oil companies came to Cleveland to refine their products. There were no clean water laws and nothing to stop industry from dumping oil, metal, paint and gasoline into the river at the time.

The first known river blaze occurred in 1868, but if there were any photos or news stories about it, they have been lost in time. Or maybe business was so good that no one thought it was important enough to record. More fires occurred in 1883 and 1887. Again, there are no stories of either fire in the papers.

By 1900, the Cuyahoga was a "rainbow of many colors." Men like John D. Rockefeller and other business magnates thought that "a dirty river was the sign of prosperity."

The most horrific recorded fire took five men's lives. It happened in 1912 when a barge at the Jefferson Avenue docks was being fueled from a gasoline tank on the bank. Oil leaked onto the surface of the river and ignited. The flames spread fast, setting Barge No. 88, which belonged to the Standard Oil Company, ablaze. The barge erupted in a huge explosion, burning to death Lewis Gale, his son Frank, Felix Boucher, Nelson Levere and Albert Marquis. They had been caulking another barge beside the first one when the flames engulfed them. All five victims were employed by the Great Lakes Towing Company.

The blaze spread over the surface of the polluted river and set fire to the tug *Wisconsin* and destroyed it. The tugs *Annie Martin* and *Pennsylvania*, at the dock opposite the burning barge, suffered substantial damage. All three vessels were owned by the Great Lakes Towing Company. A second Standard Oil barge was also destroyed in the fire. Docks owned by the Great Lakes Towing Company, Grasselli Chemical Company and Standard Oil were all heavily damaged. The total monetary loss was estimated at $450,000.

In the 1930s, most Clevelanders worked in factories in the industrial Flats. Fires on the river were so commonplace that companies and workers mostly just looked at them as a nuisance—unless they became involved.

As the population grew, sewage became a problem. An article written by Lorraine Boissoneault in *Smithsonian Magazine*, "The Cuyahoga River Caught Fire at Least a Dozen Times, but No One Cared Until 1969," reported that as early as the 1870s, the waste materials in the river were already threatening the water supply. During the 1920s, people began to complain that the water had a medicinal taste. Water department engineers did tests and found that "the polluted water of the Cuyahoga River reached the water works intakes, and this polluted water contained the material which caused the obnoxious taste."

Later, the automobile industries from both Akron and Cleveland joined in dumping their waste materials into the water.

A river fire in 1936 took several fire companies to prevent flames from traveling to eighty thousand barrels of gasoline owned by Gulf Refining Company. The fuel was stored in two tanks close to the Erie Railroad bridge. At the time, the fire came as close as fifty yards to the gasoline. The fire started in the dark, oily scum on the water's surface. A brisk breeze added to the difficulty of fighting the fire, as the blaze swept toward the bridge where the gasoline was stored. The fire began at the twelve-foot-high wooden, oil-soaked abutment, disabling the jackknife bridge. The bridge was raised to prevent the fire from spreading to the ties.

The main lines of the railroad were blocked, so all train traffic was stopped. An Erie Express train carrying forty passengers was forced to lay over. Its passengers were offloaded and taken into the city by cabs.

Seeing the possibility of a catastrophe, fire chief James E. Granger ordered all available fire apparatus to the scene. Firemen then blanketed the river with fire retardant chemicals to keep the flames away from the gasoline.

At first, the firemen were not sure how the blaze started, but they suspected it began from either smoldering waste or a spark from a blowtorch used by John Hanzel. Hanzel was working on dismantling the *Spokane*, a scrapped freighter. The thirty-six-year-old was working on the vessel's rudder when flames burst out beneath him. He fell into the river, but his fellow workers acted fast to haul him aboard the freighter. The metal sides of the boat were licked by flames, but the old craft received no damage.

It took ninety minutes for the fire department to gain control of the blaze and finally extinguish it. Chief Granger told the papers that the fire demonstrated the need for fire boat protection. The fire boats had been discontinued to save money. Damage to the bridge abutment was estimated to be $10,000.

In 1941, an ore freighter named *Negaunee* sustained $12,000 in damages from a fire on the oil-slick Cuyahoga River. The flames erupted when workmen, who were making repairs to the boat, dumped hot ashes from the stove overboard. The boat was owned by the Cleveland Cliffs Company.

The most expensive fire (moneywise) occurred on Saturday, November 1, 1952, when the oily scum on the surface of the water caught fire. The Jefferson River bridge was involved and had to be closed. The flames swept across the toxic water to the shipyard that belonged to the Great Lakes Towing Company, damaging the floating dry dock, as well as two buildings in the shipyard. Three tugboats, the *Michigan*, the *Arizona* and the *Wyoming*, were nearly destroyed.

It took at least a quarter of the city's firefighting equipment and manpower to bring the fire under control before it could spread to the Standard Oil plant, an area that contained gasoline and oil storage tanks. Company officials estimated damages to the boats, the buildings and the dry dock at $1.5 million ($12.5 million in today's money).

Two years later, the Great Lakes Towing Company sued the Standard Oil Company of Ohio for $313,000 in federal court. The towing company claimed the 1952 fire was caused by the oily surface that came from Standard Oil refining. Great Lakes Towing Company charged that the screening device the oil company had installed failed to keep the industrial waste materials from spilling into the river.

Up until 1969, the burning river was almost a joke. "You sure didn't want to fall into that s---. It'd strip your skin right off. It'd be a trip to the hospital, that's for sure," a retired ironworker said.

He was right. The river was so toxic, so polluted, the water so murky, the oil slicks so large that it bubbled with a chocolate-colored poison scum. The poison had killed the Cuyahoga River. The water was dead. The river had no oxygen, and that meant no animal or plant life could live. Not even leeches and sludge worms could live in it, according to the Federal Water Pollution Control Administration in 1969. "It oozes rather than flows," a Friday, August 1, 1969 *Time* article said. It was not unusual for workers to see the bloated bodies of rats and other small animals floating down the river. The one-hundred-mile-long Cuyahoga River was one of the worst-polluted rivers in Ohio.

According to an article in the June 21, 2019 *National Geographic* by Tim Folger, Mayor Frank Jackson remembered the neighborhoods around the river. He told Folger that the houses around the Flats had turned orange from the pollutants that poured out of industry's smokestacks.

While the industrialists shook their heads about the economic and life losses to the fires, no one was talking about the toll on the river itself. In the beginning, it was more important to attract industry and keep it booming. Industry along the Cuyahoga River was at the heart of the city's—if not the whole county's—economy.

But finally, those 1969 flames on the river helped to spark a national movement. A few days after the fire, Dr. Emmett Arnold, director of the Ohio Department of Health and also the chairman of the Ohio Water Pollution Control Board, launched an investigation into the fire and the toxicity of the river. Mayor Carl B. Stokes was fully onboard. Stokes visited the site and held a press conference the day after the fire. "What a terrible reflection on our city," he told the media.

Stokes was a trailblazer, the first Black mayor of a major city, so the media kept him in its sights. After the press conference, he asked the state to revoke any permits from companies that had previously been given permission to dump their waste materials in the Cuyahoga. He also asked the state for assistance in cleaning up the river.

Earlier that year, Santa Barbara, California, was dealing with a horrific oil spill that killed thousands of marine animals and birds. The media covered it thoroughly. Coupled with Santa Barbara's difficulties, news of a fire on the Cuyahoga River was the spark that started a new era in environmentalism. The first Earth Day was already in preparation and took place on April 22, 1970. Congress created the Environmental Protection Agency (EPA) on December 2, 1970, and passed the Clean Water Act in 1972. Louis Stokes, Ohio's first Black congressman and Carl's brother, voted for both pieces of legislation.

Fifty years have passed since the commitment to clean up the Cuyahoga. Life has slowly come back to the river. The Flats is now home to an entertainment district with restaurants, bars and nightclubs. Tall condos afford beautiful lake views. An estimated seventy species of fish now swim in the water. On a summer's day, fishermen sit along the bank with their poles dangling in the water. People kayak and paddleboard. Herons can be seen along the water's edge, and eagles have once again built their nests along the river's banks.

There is certainly more to do, but the winding Cuyahoga River is on the mend and in much better shape now than it was in 1969.

As for the term "burning river"? At least ninety businesses with those words in their names are registered with the secretary of state.

Chapter 12

MUSEUM'S *THE THINKER* VANDALIZED

Sculpture, Ohio, Spring 1970
by Mary Turzillo

March 23rd, late enough to be the 24th,
a mile away, I heard the boom,
called the cops to find out what happened.
It was The Thinker
in front of Cleveland Art Museum,
blown all to hell,
legs blasted.
Who set the dynamite?
Weathermen? or wacko kids?
Bronze doesn't talk.

In the wee hours of March 24, 1970, an unknown person(s) slipped up to the front of the Cleveland Museum of Art at 11150 East Boulevard in the Wade Park District of University Circle and planted a bomb on the marble pedestal that supported Rodin's *The Thinker*.

Red flashes lit up Severance Hall and other museums around the circle. The explosion could be heard for two miles. Police patrolling in the area heard the blast and rushed to the scene. Exercising extreme caution, they searched the area for other bombs but found none.

No one was injured, but the explosion knocked the nude, nine-hundred-pound, six-foot bronze sculpture of a man deep in contemplation to the ground. It destroyed the statue's lower legs and blew its feet off completely. The blast was so powerful it shattered six windows, dented one of the museum's huge bronze doors and took chunks out of the marble pillars and railings. Shrapnel from *The Thinker* was blown as far as five hundred feet away.

During their investigation, police found a length of pipe filled with an unknown explosive that was equivalent to three sticks of dynamite. They also found the burned remains of a ten-foot-long fuse. The fuse was similar to what the military used because it would burn at the rate of one foot per forty-five seconds, long enough to give the bomber(s) at least seven and a half minutes to get away safely.

Police spoke with the security guard who was on duty, as well as college students who were in the area, but no one had seen anything suspicious.

A message reading, "Off the ruling class" had been spray painted on *The Thinker*'s base. Political and social unrest were probably connected to

In 1970, *The Thinker* was heavily damaged by a bomb outside the Cleveland Museum of Art.

the vandalism, but the museum had not received any threats prior to the blast. Authorities suspected either Weather Underground or Students for a Democratic Society (SDS), both radical groups that were active in Cleveland at the time. Neither group claimed responsibility.

Sherman E. Lee was the museum director. He estimated the cost to repair *The Thinker* would be in the neighborhood of $20,000 to $25,000. Its value was thought to be $200,000. To be repaired properly, the statue would need to be sent to the Musée Rodin in Paris, where it was originally cast in 1916 under the direct supervision of Auguste Rodin (1840–1917).

A Cleveland industrialist and art patron, Ralph King, had purchased the piece for the museum at a cost of $6,500. Rodin died shortly before the museum installed it in 1917.

Eleven other castings of *The Thinker* are owned by museums in the United States. Twelve more are in museum collections around the world. All of these casts were authorized by Rodin, but fewer than ten of them were cast during Rodin's lifetime. The Cleveland Museum's is one of those ten. The original sits in the exterior gardens at the Musée Rodin.

Rodin first conceived of the sculpture in 1880. He named it *Le Poete* (*The Poet*) but changed it to *Le Poete/Le Penseur* (*The Poet/The Thinker*). Later, it became *Le Penseur—The Thinker*. It was created to be part of Rodin's monumental sculpture *The Gates of Hell*, bronze doors created for the museum in Paris. *The Gates* depicted Dante's *Inferno* (Italian for fire), the first part of the *Divine Comedy*. *The Thinker*, in his pensive pose, began as a much smaller figure to sit at the top of the gate. Sitting over the door, *The Thinker* was meant to represent Dante in deep thought.

The original was just over twenty-seven inches high. With the help of sculptor Henri Lebosse's Collas machine (similar to a pantograph) that could enlarge or reduce an item by tracing it onto another block of clay, *The Thinker* grew to his imposing size.

At first, the Cleveland Museum of Art deliberated sending the sculpture to the Musée Rodin in Paris for molds that could be cast for the damaged parts of the sculpture. Acquiring a replacement was another consideration. In the end, the museum decided to remount the sculpture and display it in its scarred form. In doing so, Rodin's original work was preserved.

In 2017, the museum received a tip on the bombing, but it went nowhere. More than fifty years later, the crime remains unsolved.

"Bronze doesn't talk."

Chapter 13

INDIANS' TEN-CENT
BEER NIGHT

The Cleveland Indians (now Cleveland Guardians) were not drawing big crowds in 1974. The Municipal Stadium where the Tribe played was built circa 1931 and designed to seat more than seventy-eight thousand fans. Due to population and business loss and plain old lack of interest, the team was lucky to draw four thousand at that time.

Indians executive vice president Ted Bonda determined something needed to be done and began to look for ways to bring the crowds back. One of his staff came up with the idea of a Ten-Cent Beer Night, citing the Texas Rangers' recent success with it. The premise sounded good, so plans were set into action for a Ten-Cent Beer Night on June 4, when the Indians would meet the Rangers in Cleveland.

Bad blood flowed between the teams, but apparently Bonda's staff gave no thought to that. The last time the teams played, which was at the end of May, they met out on the Texas field, where Rangers fans threw beer and food at the Indians. Fights broke out that night, and the tribe lost that game 3–0.

Understandably, Clevelanders did not respond well to the chant "mistake by the lake," so they were not in a good mood when the Rangers came to town to play ball. Adding fuel to the fire, the Rangers' manager Billy Martin told the press he was not worried about any retaliation from Cleveland fans over the previous game because the Tribe did not have enough fans to retaliate. Radio 3WE sports personality Pete Franklin stoked the fire. By the time the Rangers hit town, Cleveland was ready.

An advertisement for the Indians' Ten-Cent Beer Night. *Author's collection.*

On that sweltering evening with a full moon, 25,134 fans showed up, and they started to chug sixty thousand cans of beer. Some fans were already plastered when they got there, if not from booze, from weed. Adding to the suds, several hundred fans came ready to light up the night with firecrackers. What could possibly go wrong?

By the second inning, the Rangers were leading, and the crowd was half in the bag. One hefty female fan apparently thought she could offer the Indians some incentive, so she climbed over the wall, rushed up to the Indians' on-deck circle and tore open her blouse to expose her ample breasts. Then she ran over and tried to kiss umpire Nestor Chylak, but he fought her off.

Home field fans were just warming up by the top of the fifth. Every time a Ranger stepped up to the plate, Cleveland fans booed him. When Tom Grieve hit a second home run, a naked man came out of nowhere and streaked across the field, then slid into second. No comment on that, except it seemed to be the inspiration for two more men to plunge over the wall and moon the Texas outfield.

The crowd was on a roll when the Tribe's Leron Lee smacked a line drive straight at Rangers pitcher Fergie Jenkins. Jenkins did not move out of the way fast enough, and the ball hit him square in the stomach. While Jenkins writhed in agony, fans chanted, "Hit him again harder! Harder!"

A bit later, Martin got into an argument with the umpire over a close call at third. To show their disgust for him, Cleveland fans pelted him with cups of beer. In response, Martin blew kisses into the stands.

Things escalated from there. Gangs of drunken fans got down on the field and played their own game of catch with a tennis ball. Ushers and security ran them off. Those who couldn't get down on the field continued to throw beer cups, food wrappers—anything they could get their hands on—onto the field. All the while, the announcers pleaded with people not to litter.

Meanwhile, concession stands were running out of beer. Someone decided to detour Cleveland's thirsty fans to the Stroh's trucks parked behind the outfield fence.

Back in the game, the Rangers were winning by two runs. In 1974, Mike Hargrove was playing first base for Texas. He dodged a fifth of Thunderbird

Crowds at the Indians' dugout on the Ten-Cent Beer Night. *Author's collection.*

aimed at his head. Someone tossed firecrackers into the Rangers' bullpen. Fans began ripping down the padding off the outfield wall.

Just as the Tribe tied the game with two runs in the ninth and stood to win with a runner on second, a guy bolted onto the field and reached for Rangers outfielder Jeff Burroughs's cap. The Texan turned in reaction but tripped.

Seeing this, Martin thought Burroughs needed help, and he had had enough. He grabbed a bat and yelled to his players, "Let's go get 'em, boys." The team followed orders. Bats in hand, they charged onto the field but quickly realized they were outnumbered. Their bats were no match for the knives and chains in the hands of a plastered gang of Cleveland fans.

Indians manager Ken Aspromonte saw what was happening and decided it was time to exercise professional courtesy and back up the Rangers. He and the rest of the Tribe took up their bats and stormed the field. It was an all-out rumble. Police and security waded into the fray, and players escaped into dugouts.

When the crowd realized the players were gone and the police meant business, they begrudgingly dispersed. Before they left the field, they stole all the bases and anything that wasn't nailed down.

Chylak, wiping the blood from a cut on his head, knew there was no use to field the teams again and called the game. The Indians had to forfeit.

Afterward, in the locker room, the Indians seemed to be in shock. Relief pitcher Tom Hilgendorf, who got hit in the back of the head with a flying chair, said he saw trouble brewing as early as the fourth. Pitcher Jim Perry had been in the thick of it: "Everybody was pushing everybody." He said left-fielder Alex Johnson and catcher Duke Sims were "mad, real mad.…But we started back to the dugout, thinking it might be over. Then here came some more and then we had it all over again."

Shortstop Frank Duffy said, "If [only] the fans would have had sense enough to hold back and let us win." He shook his head. "This was the worst I've ever seen. So much for Ten-Cent Beer Night."

Epilogue

IN PLAIN SIGHT

The best place to hide is in plain sight. Fugitive Ted Conrad followed that advice for more than half a century. The handsome, charming Conrad had been wanted for embezzlement ever since a few days after he turned twenty.

In 1969, he worked as a vault teller at the Society National Bank in downtown Cleveland. A graduate of Lakewood High School, he was smart, and with an IQ of 135, he learned quickly. His boss and co-workers said he was going places. Little did they know where.

On Friday, July 11—the day after his twentieth birthday—he came back from his lunch break with a paper sack containing a fifth of Canadian Club and a carton of Marlboros. He made a point of showing his purchase to the security guard and joked about how he was going to party over the weekend for his birthday.

At closing time, Conrad told his vault partner to go ahead on out and he would be right along. His boss was in the hospital, so Ted was then alone in the vault. When he left the bank, he stopped to talk to the vice president of operations. After a bit, he smiled and waved at security and walked out of the bank carrying his sack of Canadian Club and Marlboros. No one suspected that stuffed in around the bottle of booze and the smokes were $50 and $100 bills totaling $215,000.

The theft was not noticed until the following Monday, when the young vault teller did not report for work. The FBI was not called until the day after that.

Soon after the authorities got involved, Conrad was indicted for embezzlement (not robbery) and falsifying bank records. The indictment meant the statute of limitations would never run out. Conrad was a fugitive from justice, a wanted man.

Except for a possible sighting in Hawaii, which was never confirmed, he was never seen or heard from again. Federal investigators followed up on leads from Washington, D.C., to cities across the country to Los Angeles. Conrad was fluent in French, so Canada and French-speaking countries came to mind. Authorities also followed up on a tip in England. But they were all dead ends. Television shows such as *Unsolved Mysteries* and *America's Most Wanted* turned up nothing.

The trail went cold.

I wrote about Ted Conrad in my 2021 book *Ohio Heists: Historic Bank Holdups, Train Robberies, Jewel Stings and More.* Out of all the thieves in that

One of the few photos of young Ted Conrad. *U.S. Marshals Service, Cleveland Office.*

book, he was the most interesting to me. He got away with it.

His close friend from high school, Russell Metcalf, told me in an interview that Conrad was obsessed with the 1968 movie *The Thomas Crown Affair*, which starred Steve McQueen. McQueen played the part of a bored millionaire who entertained himself by plotting a bank robbery. Conrad watched that movie at least six times. According to friends, he was preoccupied with Thomas Crown and began to emulate him by dressing like him, driving a sports car and playing pool and golf. He liked the idea of deception and even went so far as to shoplift, according to Metcalf. He told friends how easy it would be to steal from the bank and get away with it. "He talked about how loose security was at the bank," Metcalf said. "I think he wanted to prove he could do it."

After a half century, the case still haunted retired deputy marshal John K. Elliott, who was involved in the case at the beginning. He knew it was not going to be easy because the bank had bonded Conrad but never fingerprinted him. After retiring, Elliott stayed informed on the hunt through his son U.S. marshal Peter J. Elliott, who now heads up the Northern District of Ohio.

In 2019, I interviewed both Elliotts for *Ohio Heists.* The elder Elliott was adamant that Conrad would be found someday. He said the warrant for Conrad's arrest belonged to him. He took a special interest in the case because he and his family lived close to the Conrads. They frequented a neighborhood ice cream store where Conrad worked. They even went to the same doctor.

The question remained, after all those years, was he still alive? At the time I interviewed the Elliotts, they both thought so. "It's a gut feeling," Peter J. Elliott said. "He's probably had a good life. He had all that money. He probably got married and has a family. He probably had a whole different identity and his family doesn't even know who he is. He's the only one who knows. He was smart and educated." Little did he know.

Conrad's trail stayed cold until November 2, 2021, when I got an email.

Sometimes I get emails about my various books or my blog or presentations. But the one I got on that morning was much different. It asked if I was interested in information about Ted Conrad. Not knowing who this person was or what was behind the information, I was leery but intrigued, so I wrote back and said "yes." In response, the person sent me an obituary for a man named Thomas Randele who had lived and died in Lynnfield, Massachusetts, north of Boston. The obituary featured a photo of a smiling older man. I did not recognize the man's name or the picture.

But I began to read. Randele's birth date (July 10, 1947) matched Ted Conrad's, except for the year; Conrad was born in 1949. The birthplace of Denver, Colorado, matched. Randele's parents' names were Edward and Ruthabeth (maiden name Krueger). His mother's name was a dead giveaway. It was an uncommon name, and it was Conrad's mother's name.

The rest of the obituary all fit. Thomas Randele attended New England College; so did Conrad. Conrad's father taught political science there. Randele had been a golf pro and sold expensive cars. Conrad was known to be good at golf, and just like Thomas Crown, he enjoyed expensive sports cars. Beyond those things, Randele had been married and had a family.

Was this obituary too good to be true? I dug out my original file and found Russell Metcalf's contact. I sent him the obituary to see if he could recognize Conrad from the picture. He wasn't 100 percent sure, but he thought it was Ted Conrad. The source sent a photo of Conrad's brother alongside Randele's obituary photo. The resemblance was stunning.

After that, I started scrolling through social media and found pictures of when Randele was younger. At that point, there was no doubt. It was Ted Conrad. The person who sent me the obituary had tried to contact law enforcement but got no response. I knew who would respond.

The next morning, I emailed the obituary to U.S. marshal Peter J. Elliott and told him what I had found on social media. When we spoke on the

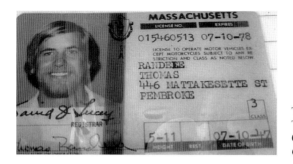

The 1970s driver's license of Thomas Randele, alias of Ted Conrad. *U.S. Marshals Service, Cleveland Office.*

phone a short time later, he said he thought it was Conrad, but he would have to confirm it. I thought perhaps he meant DNA, but he would not say one way or the other.

Marshal Elliott traveled to Lynnfield to talk to the family. He learned Conrad had eluded authorities by reinventing himself. According to street directories, he had lived in the Boston area since 1970, six months after the theft. Using his new identity, he walked into a Social Security Administration office and asked for an identification number and card with his new name. He gave his birth year as 1947 instead of 1949 but kept the date the same. Back then, people usually did not get their Social Security cards until they were adults, so no one at the administration office questioned him. After that, he got a driver's license, opened a bank account and got a job.

He met his wife, Kathy, soon after landing in Boston, but they did not get married until 1982. He was a good father and husband—an upstanding citizen of Lynnfield. "From what I learned, he was a great family man," Elliott said. "He was even friends with the police in the area, and from my understanding, he was friends with federal agents in the area." Elliott also said Randele/Conrad enjoyed watching true crime television.

According to an Associated Press article by John Seewer and Jennifer McDermott, Conrad had a number of golfing pals and former co-worker friends. His buddies said he was well spoken, polite and a "gentle soul." He did not drink much, and he seldom got upset.

"Nobody knew his true identity," Marshal Pete Elliott said. His friends were stunned when they found out, but they thought back on how he always wore a beard and glasses and never talked about his past.

Conrad might have chosen the Boston vicinity because that is where *The Thomas Crown Affair* was filmed. He obviously chose the first name Thomas from the title character. Steve McQueen had portrayed Josh Randall in a television series, *Wanted Dead or Alive*. Perhaps Conrad took that last name and gave it a slight twist. We will never know.

In good weather, he played professional golf in and around Boston. He took his game to Florida in the winter months. He worked at Pembroke Country Club in Pembroke as a golf pro and then as full-time manager of the club. He was so good at golf that he outplayed Hall of Famer Johnny Miller during a charity outing. He later sold expensive foreign automobiles.

The $215,000 (now worth approximately $1.7 million) apparently did not go far. Who knows how he spent it? Maybe he blew it, or maybe he lived on it, or maybe he invested poorly. The marshals are looking into what became of it as of this writing.

By 2014, the money was not enough to keep him and his family out of bankruptcy in Boston Federal Court. The filing showed they owed $160,000 in credit card debt and had few assets. The U.S. marshals confirmed his identity by matching the signatures on his 1967 college application with the 2014 bankruptcy papers.

Sadly, John Elliott never saw Ted Conrad apprehended, as Elliott passed away in 2020. However, his collection of the college documents is what confirmed Conrad's identity. It was fitting that his son was the one to use those documents.

Conrad's mother, father and beloved grandmother always thought that someone put him up to the embezzlement and that he was dead. They all died without knowing the truth. Oddly, he was not listed as a family member in any of their obituaries.

Conrad died as Thomas Randele on May 18, 2021, of lung cancer. The disease robbed him of his voice, so he could not visit with his many friends at the end.

He was on his deathbed when he told his family who he really was and what he had done. His wife declined to talk to journalists, except to say that her husband "was a great man."

In all those years, his family had no idea that he was really fugitive Ted Conrad, and he was hiding in plain sight.

BIBLIOGRAPHY

Sᴇх, Vɪᴄᴇ ᴀɴᴅ Rᴏᴄᴋ-ᴀɴᴅ-Rᴏʟʟ

Books and Periodicals

Collins, Max Allan, and A. Brad Schwartz. *Eliot Ness and the Mad Butcher: Hunting America's Deadliest Unidentified Serial Killer*. New York: HarperCollins, 2020.

Dutka, Alan F. *Cleveland's Short Vincent: The Theatrical Grill and Its Notorious Neighbors*. Cleveland: Cleveland Landmarks Press, Inc., 2012.

Karpis, Alvin, with Bill Trent. *The Alvin Karpis Story*. Repr., New York: Ishi Press, 2011.

Nickel, Steven. *Torso: The Story of Eliot Ness and the Search for a Psychopathic Killer*. Winston-Salem, NC: John F. Blair, Publisher, 1989.

O'Brien, Erin, and Bob Perkoski. *Rust Belt Burlesque: The Softer Side of a Heavy Metal Town*. Athens: Swallow Press/Ohio University Press, 2019.

Petkovic, John. "Cleveland's Legendary Roxy and the Burlesque Geyday." *Plain Dealer*, May 18, 2016, updated May 19, 2019.

Schwartz, Ted. *Cleveland Curiosities: Eliot Ness & His Blundering Raid, a Busker's Promise, the Richest Heiress Who Never Lived and More*. Charleston, SC: The History Press, 2010.

Skanse, Richard. "Plasmatics' Wendy O. Williams Commits Suicide." *Rolling Stone*, April 9, 1998.

Variety Staff. "Wendy O. Williams Dies at 48." *Variety Magazine*, April 16, 1998.

Newspapers

Associated Press
Cleveland Leader
New York Times
Norfolk [OH] Reflector Herald
Plain Dealer (Cleveland, OH)
Register-Recorder (Rockford, IL)
Times Recorder (Zanesville, OH)

Websites

"Eliot Ness, the Harvard Club." sites.google.com/site/onamissionrevived/ eliotness-theharvardclub.

Encyclopedia of Cleveland History. "Harvard Club." case.edu/ech/ articles/h/harvard-club.

———. "Hollenden Hotel." case.edu/ech/articles/h/hollendenhotel.

———. "Levine, Manuel V." case.edu/ech/articles/l/levin-manuel-v.

———. "Roxy Theater." case.edu/ech/articles/r/roxy-theater.

———. "Short Vincent." case.edu/ech/articles/s/shortvincent.

FBI/Vault. vault.fbi.gov/Eliot%20Ness/Eliot%20Ness%20Part%201%20 of%205.

Hannan, Sheehan. "1943: Police Raid a Porn Den." *Cleveland Magazine*, March 30, 2017. clevelandmagazine.com/in-the-cle/terminal/articles/1943-police-raid-a-porn-den.

———. "Then & Now: Short Vincent." *Cleveland Magazine*, November 25, 2015. clevelandmagazine.com/in-the-cle/articles/then-now-short-vincent.

Marcus, Jim. "A Remarkable Memory." Ohioburlesque.com.

Miller, Marilyn. "Short Vincent." Cleveland Historical, February 22, 2010. clevelandhistorical.org/items/show/64.

Mossbrook, Joe. "Jazzed in Cleveland, Part 93, the Theatrical Grill." wmv_ news/jazz93.htm.

Newbold, Allison V. "Hollenden Hotel." Cleveland Historical. clevelandhistorical. org/Items/show/818.

Red Hots: Variety and Cabaret. "Legend: Carrie Finnell." redhotsburlesque. com/2013/legend-carrie-finnell.

Roy, Chris. "The Theatrical Grill." Cleveland Historical. clevelandhistorical. org/items/show/906.

www.cleveland.com.

Cops, Corpses and Crooks

Books and Periodicals

Adler, William M. *The Man Who Never Died: The Life, Times, and Legacy of Joe Hill, American Labor Icon*. New York: Bloomsbury USA, 2011.

Baranick, Alana, Jim Sheeler and Stephen Miller. *Life on the Death Beat: A Handbook for Obituary Writers*. Oak Park, IL: Marion Street Press, 2005.

Bayne, Neil F., and Wes Sarginson. *Fast Eddie*. New York: Leisure Books, 1983.

Condon, George E. *Cleveland: The Best Kept Secret*. Garden City, NY, 1967.

Dennis, Howard. "Emma Goldman and the Cleveland Anarchists." *Modern Culture*, November 1901.

Domm, Sally. "With Death, You Talk Softly." *Plain Dealer*, September 17, 1978.

Greenhouse, Steven. "Examining a Labor Hero's Death." *New York Times*, August 26, 2011.

Harvey, Tom. "If Not Joe Hill, Who Killed the Morrisons?" *Salt Lake Tribune*, November 15, 2015.

Howard, N.R. "I, Fred Kohler" series. *Plain Dealer*, February–March 1934.

Kenney, Christopher. *The McKinley Monument: A Tribute to a Fallen President*. Charleston, SC: The History Press, 2006.

Mio, Lou. "The Anarchist Who Killed McKinley." *Plain Dealer*, February 3, 1991.

Morten, James "Big Jim," and David G. Wittels. "I Was King of Thieves," 3-part series. *Saturday Evening Post*, August 5, 12, 19, 1950.

Rauchway, Eric. *Murdering McKinley*. New York: Hill and Wang, 2003.

Schwartz, Ted. *Cleveland Curiosities: Eliot Ness & His Blundering Raid, a Busker's Promise, the Richest Heiress Who Never Lived and More*. Charleston, SC: The History Press, 2010.

Newspapers

Akron Beacon Journal
Associated Press
Battle Creek [MI] Enquirer
Canton Repository
Capital Times (Madison, WI)

Cincinnati Enquirer
Cincinnati Post
Cleveland Leader
Cleveland Press
Columbus Dispatch
Dayton Daily News
Detroit Free Press
Greenville [OH] Daily Advocate
Lansing [MI] State Journal
Los Angeles Times
Marion [OH] Star
Minneapolis Star
Newark [OH] Advocate
St. Louis Globe-Democrat
Tribune (Coshocton, OH)
Wisconsin State Journal

Websites

Baehr, Hermann C. case.edu/ech/articles/b/baehr-hermann.
Encyclopedia of Cleveland History. "Czologsz, Leon F." case.edu/ech/articles/c/czolgosz-leon-f.
———. "Franklin Club." case.edu/ech/articles/f/franklin-club.
———. "Kohler, Frederick." case.edu/ech/articles/k/kohler-frederick.
Find a Grave. www.findagrave.com/memorial/31993456/john-leonard-whitfield.
Markel, Howard. "Would McKinley Have Survived an Assassin's Bullet If He Had a Different Doctor?" *PBS NewsHour*, February 14, 2019. www.pbs.org/newshour/health/would-mckinley-have-survived-an-assassins-bullet-if-he-had-a-different-doctor.
Records of Convictions. *The State of Ohio v. 17269 James Morton*. Common Pleas Court Criminal Journal 30, 17.
United States Federal Census 1920.
Winter, Jim. "Fast Eddie." www.sleuthsayers.org.

BLAZES, BOMBS AND BEER

Books and Periodicals

"America's Sewage System and the Price of Optimism." *Time*, August 1, 1969.

Boissoneault, Lorraine. "The Cuyahoga River Caught Fire at Least a Dozen Times, but No One Cared Until 1969." *Smithsonian Magazine*, June 19, 2019.

Condon, George E. "Some Thought on *The Thinker*." *Plain Dealer*, April 22, 1970.

Floger, Tim. "The Cuyahoga River Caught Fire 50 Years Ago. It Inspired a Movement." *National Geographic*, June 21, 2019.

Heaton, Michael. "Dan Coughlin Recalls the Indians' Famous Ten-Cent Beer Night." *Plain Dealer*, June 4, 2014.

Jackson, Paul. "The Night Beer and Violence Bubbled Over in Cleveland." Espn.com, May 28, 2008.

Litt, Steven. "Cleveland Museum of Art Shared Tip about 1970 Bombing of Rodin 'Thinker' with FBI." Cleveland.com, August 31, 2017.

Roy, Chris. "Cleveland's Philosopher King." Clevelandhistorical.org/items/show/575.

Sanchez, Lisa. "The Death and Life of a Statue: How *The Thinker* Was Reborn in Cleveland." Cleveland Public Library, December 22, 2017.

Smith, Julie Carr, and Tony Dejak. "Burning River Loses Sting in Cleveland 50 Years After Fire." ABC News, June 18, 2019.

Newspapers

Abilene [TX] Reporter-News
Akron Beacon Journal
Alliance [OH] Review
Canton Repository
Cincinnati Enquirer
Cleveland Press
Dayton Daily News
Journal Herald (Dayton, OH)
News-Journal (Mansfield, OH)
Piqua [OH] Daily Call

Plain Dealer (Cleveland, OH)
State Times Advocate (Baton Rouge, LA)
Times Herald (Port Huron, MI)
Times Recorder (Zanesville, OH)

Websites

Cleveland Museum of Art. "Rodin's *The Thinker.*" Clevelandart.org/research/conservation/rodins-thinker.
———. "*The Thinker* Vandalized." Clevelandart.org/research/library/how-to-research/rodins-the-thinker/vandalized.
"History of the Cuyahoga River." www.grc.nasa.gov/www/K-12/fenlewis/History.html.
National Park Service. "The Cuyahoga, a National Heritage Rivere." www.nps.gov/articles/000/cuyahoga-national-heritage-river.htm.
Ohio History Central. "Cuyahoga River Fire." Ohiohistorycentral.org/w/Cuyahoga_River_Fire.
Rodin Museum. www.rodinmusem.org.
Turzillo, Mary. "Sculpture, Ohio, Spring 1970." Newversenews, May 11, 2009. newversenews.blogspot.com/2009/05/sculpture-ohio-spring-1970.html.

E<small>PILOGUE</small>

"Obituary for Thomas Randele." hosting-6792.tributes.com/obituary/show/Thomas-Randele-108518750.
Seewer, John, and Jennifer McDermott. "Friendly Family Man's 50-Year Secret: He Was a Fugitive, Too." Associated Press, December 29, 2021.
Turzillo, Jane Ann. *Ohio Heists: Historic Bank Holdups, Train Robberies, Jewel Stings and More.* Charleston, SC: The History Press, 2021.
U.S. Marshals Service News Release. "One of America's Most Wanted Fugitives Identified after 52 Years." November 12, 2021.

ABOUT THE AUTHOR

Author Jane Ann Turzillo is a multi–National Federation of Press Women award winner for her books and journalism. She has been nominated twice for the Agatha for her books *Wicked Women of Ohio* (2018) and *Unsolved Murders & Disappearances in Northeast Ohio* (2016), both published by The History Press. A full-time author and speaker, she concentrates on vintage true crimes and history. As one of the original owners of a large weekly newspaper, she covered police, fire and hard news. Before she turned to writing books, she wrote short stories and articles that were published in newspapers and magazines across the United States and Canada. She is a graduate of The University of Akron with degrees in criminal justice technology and mass-media communication. She is a member of National Federation of Press Women, Society of Professional Journalists, Mystery Writers of America and Sisters in Crime. Visit her website at www.janeannturzillo.com and read her blog at darkheartedwomen.wordpress.com.

Visit us at
www.historypress.com